TRAINING AND DEVELOPMENT

TRAINING AND DEVELOPMENT

SONAL BIST

Lecturer

Shri Guru Ram Rai Institute of
Technology and Science,
Dehradun

AN ISO 9001:2008 CERTIFIED COMPANY

VAYU EDUCATION OF INDIA

2/25, Ansari Road, Darya Ganj, New Delhi-110 002

Training and Development

ISBN: 978-93-80712-46-8

First Edition: 2010
Reprint: 2013

Rs. 125.00

Printed & bound in India

Published by:

AN ISO 9001:2008 CERTIFIED COMPANY

VAYU EDUCATION OF INDIA

2/25, Ansari Road, Darya Ganj, New Delhi-110 002
Ph.: 91-11-47236600, 41564445
Fax: 91-11-41564440
E-mail: vei@veiindia.com
Web: www.veiindia.com

Dedicated
to
My Loving
SHAURYA & AANYA

Preface

The concept of training and development assumes immense importance as training and development plays a vital role in meeting the challenging requirements of the organizations and also of the highly skilled and competent human resources due to globalization.

This book contains a comprehensive discussion of the elements of training and development. Training is helpful in developing the human resources and Human beings are a resource to an organization. There is a fundamental truth that "people are an organization's most important asset". In every organization, human resources are a pivotal variable without which the in animate assets are worthless. Like cash put into a savings account, human resources also appreciate in value. Therefore, human resources need to be understood in there proper perspective and utilized effectively to achieve the goals of an organization. This requires that human resources must be enhanced through training and development.

The management of human resources is very complicated and challenging task for those who are entrusted with successful running of an organization; and this implies considerable knowledge of various aspects of training and development like its objectives, principles. Process, techniques and finally the evaluation of the training programmes in order to check the effectiveness of training.

In fact, the differences in the level of economic development of the countries are largely a reflection of the differences in the quality of their human resources. Therefore, in order to upgrade and develop our human resources it is of immense importance that we provide training on a regular basis and evaluate the employee's performance in order to realize the benefits of training.

—Sonal Bist

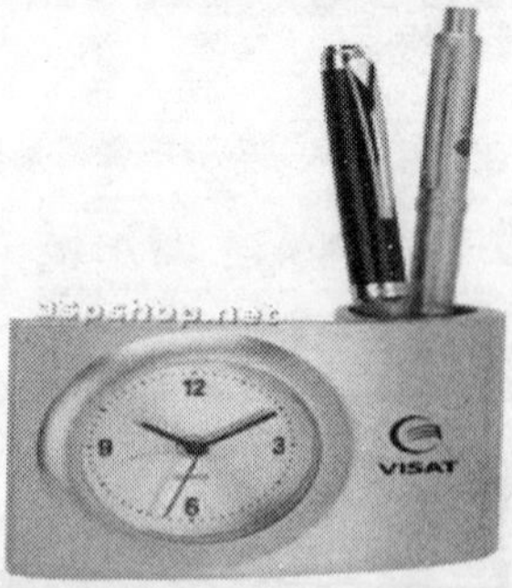

Acknowledgement

Every author owes a great deal to others and the author of this book is no exception. First and foremost I would like to express to my sincere thanks to my gurus, who nurtured and groomed me through my formative years and continue to motivate me to keep learning throughout the journey of life. I would like to thank my parents *Mrs. Nirupma* and *Mr. Vijendra Singh Bist* and my family members without whom I would not have been what I am today. I would also like to express to my sincere thanks to *Dr. Raina* (Director, SGRRITS) for his constant support. I also thank the Almighty, without whose blessings and grace this challenging task could not have been accomplished.

Though it is difficult to thank everyone individually, it is my pleasure to express my gratitude to Dr. Rajeev Kumar Jain (Managing Director), Prof. Sanjeev Kumar Sharma (Chairperson) of Vayu Education of India, Darya Ganj, New Delhi. I would also like to thank Mr. Vijay Kumar Saini (Production Manager), Mr. Jitender Kumar Sharma (Sr. Sales Executive) and other production team members of Vayu Education of India, who published the book within a short duration in order to deliver a good quality book for the students who will really be benefited when they go through this book.

This book has become a reality because of the extreme love and continuous encouragement of my colleagues and all my near and dear ones. I take this opportunity to thank *Dr. Deepak Sahni* and *Prof. A. Chatterjee* for their support and motivation. Last but not the least I would also like to thank the members of the library of SGRRITS for their enumerable help.

Special Thanks to all my *loving friends*.

—Sonal Bist

Reviewing Committee

Name	Designation
1. **Prof. Sanjeev Kumar Sharma** *Professor and Head* of Computer Science and Engg. J.P.E.I.T. Meerut	Chairman
2. **Mr. Ashok Kumar** *Asstt. Prof.* in Computer Science and Engg. GRD Institute of Technology, Dehradun	Member
3. **Sanjay Kumar** *Sr. Lecturer,* Computer Science and Engg. Roorkee Institute of Technology, Roorkee	Member
4. **Mr. Harish Sharma** *Lecturer* MCA Department, SGRRI, Dehradun	Member
5. **Anuj Pundir** *System Analyst* HCL Noida	Member
6. **Manoj Kumar Saini** *System Analyst* B.dot Software Solution, Noida	Member
7. **Amit Gupta** *Assistant Professor* JPIET, Meerut.	Member
8. **Abhinay Agarwal** *Head,* Mechanical Engineering Deptt. JPIET, Meerut.	Member

According to Prescribed Syllabus

for

B.B.A. Ist First Semester

of

H.N.B. Garhwal University (Uttrakhand)

SYLLABUS

Training and Development

COURSE CONTENTS

(i) Importance of Training, Education, Training-Employment Development Cycle, Systems Approach to Training.

(ii) Psychology of Learning and Learned Motivation, Assessment of Training Needs.

(iii) Setting of Training Objectives, Training Methods and Aids, Design of Training Programmes. Training and Trainers.

(iv) Training for Special Groups, Executive Development Programmes. Career Planning.

(v) Evaluation of Training, Training and Organization.

SUGGESTED READINGS

(1) Sonal Bist - Training and Development

(2) Singh, Chhabara and Taneja - Personnel Management and Industrial Relations

(3) Finningan, J. - Industrial Training Management

(4) Lundy, James L. - Effective Industrial Management

(5) Flippo, Edwin B. - Principles of Personnel Management

Contents

1

Training and Development

Training

INTRODUCTION

Poverty stricken India spends 45 billion each year, wealthy USA nearly twice as much. Training like a tax, has been levied on the willing and unwilling alike. In fact, some countries have made it a tax or at least expenditure strongly encouraged. French law, for example, requires factories in some industries to spend a fixed percentage of their budget on personnel training or forfeit any unspent amount in taxes; the purpose behind this policy is the equitable spread of the costs of upgrading the work force in general

Every organisation needs to have well trained and experienced people to perform the activities that have to be done. If the current or potential job occupant can meet this requirement, training is not important. But when this is not the case, it is necessary to raise the skill levels and increase the versatility and adaptability of employees. In-adequate job performance or a decline in productivity or changes resulting out of job redesigning or a technological breakthrough require some type of training and development efforts. As the job become more complex, the importance of employee development also increases. In a rapidly changing society, employee training and development are not only an activity that is desirable but also an activity that an organization must commit resources to if it is to maintain a viable and knowledgeable workforce.

After an employee is selected, placed and introduced he or she must be provided with training facilities. Training is the act of increasing the knowledge and skill of an employee for doing a particular job. Training is a short term educational process and utilizing a systematic and organized procedure by which employees learn technical knowledge and skills for a definite purpose.

In other words training improves, changes, moulds the employee's knowledge, skill, behavior, aptitude and attitude towards the requirements of the job and organization. Training refers to the teaching and learning activities carried on for the primary purpose of helping members of an organization , to acquire and apply knowledge, skills, abilities and attitudes needed by a particular job and organization .Thus , training bridges the differences between job requirements and employee's present specifications. Training is a process of learning a sequence of programmed behaviors.

Reddy (2005) has formulated the acronym of training as

T – Talent and tenacity (strong determination)

R – Reinforcement (something positive to be reinforced to memory and to the system, again and again, until it becomes a spontaneous affair)

A – Awareness (with which one takes long strides of progress)

I – Interest (which is invariably accompanied by excitement and enthusiasm)

N – Novelties (new things, the likes of which would sustain one's interest, and fill the heart with thrills and sensations).

I – Intensity (the training instilled into the trainers' mind must acquire experience – oriented intensity)

N – Nurturing (refers to incessant nurturing of talent, which otherwise would remain latent and dormant)

G – Grip (a fine grip over situations solves multiple problem and enables one to acquire a practical approach along with all the tricks and tactics, to achieve success after success in one's Endeavour's)

Thus, talent and tenacity, reinforcement, awareness, interest, novelties, intensity, nurturing and grip are the keywords conveying the flavor and fragrance of training and all its facets.

DEFINITIONS OF TRAINING

Training is "the systematic development of the knowledge, skills and attitudes required by an individual to perform adequately a given task or job". **—Armstrong**

Training is "the act of increasing knowledge and skills of an employee for doing a particular job" **—Edwin B. Flippo**

"Training is a short term process utilizing a systematic and organized procedure by which non-managerial personnel learn technical knowledge and skill for a definite purpose. Development is a long term educational process utilizing a systematic and organized procedure by which managerial personnel learn conceptual and theoretical knowledge for general purpose."

—Lawrence Steinmetz

Principles of Training

Providing training in the knowledge of different skills is a complex process. A number of principles have been involved which can be followed as guidelines by the trainees. Some of them are follows:

1. **Motivation:** As the effectiveness of an employee depends on how well he is motivated by management, the effectiveness of learning also depends on motivation. In other words, the trainee will acquire a new skill or knowledge thoroughly and quickly if he or she is highly motivated. Thus, the training must be related to the desires of the trainee such as more wages or better job, recognition, status, promotion etc.
2. **Progress Information:** It has been found through various research studies that there is a relation between learning rapidly and effectively and providing right information specifically, and as such the training should not give excessive information or information that can be misinterpreted. The trainees also want to learn a new skill without much difficulty and without handing too much or receiving excessive information or wrong type of progressive information. So, the trainer has to provide only the required amount of progressive information specifically to the trainee.
3. **Reinforcement:** The effectiveness of the trainee in learning new skills or acquiring new knowledge should be reinforced by means of rewards and punishment. Examples of positive reinforcement are promotions, rise in pay, praise etc. Punishments are also called negative reinforcement. Management should take care to reward the successful trainees.

   The management can punish the trainees whose behaviour is undesirable. But the consequences of such punishments have their long-run ill effect on the trainer as well as on the management. Hence, the management should take much care in case of negative reinforcement.
4. **Practice:** A trainee should actively participate in the training programmes in order to make them effective. Continuous and long practice is highly essential for effective learning. Jobs are broken down into elements from which the fundamental physical, sensory and mental skills are extracted. Training exercises should be provided for each skill.

5. **Full Vs. Part:** It is not clear whether it is best to teach the complete job at a stretch or dividing the job into parts and teaching each part separately at a time. If the job is complex and requires too long to learn, it is better to teach each part of the job separately and then put the parts together into an effective complete job. Generally the training process should start from the known and proceed to the unknown and from the easy to the difficult when parts are taught. However, the trainer has to teach the trainees based on his judgments on their motivation and convenience.
6. **Individual Preferences:** Individual training is costly, and group training is economically viably and advantageous to the organisation. But individuals vary in intelligence and aptitude from person to person. So the trainer has to adjust the training programme to the individual abilities and aptitude. In addition, individual teaching machines and adjustments of differences should be taken care of.

Importance of Training

Training is the corner stone of sound management for it makes employees more effective and productive. It is actively connected with all the personnel and managerial activities. The importance of human resource management to a large extent depends on human resource development. Training is the most important technique of human resource development. No organization can get a candidate who exactly matches with the job and the organizational requirements. Hence, training is important to develop the employee and make him suitable for the job. There is an ever present need for training men so that new and changed techniques may be taken advantage of and improvements affected in the old methods, which are woefully inefficient.

Training is a practical and of vital necessity because, apart from the other advantages mentioned above it enables employees to develop and rise within the organization, and increase their 'market value' 'earning power' and 'job security'. It moulds the employees' attitudes and helps them to achieve a better co-operation with the company and greater loyalty to it. The management is benefited in the sense that higher standards of quality are achieved; a satisfactory organizational structure is build up; authority can be delegated and stimulus for progress applied to employees.

Training, moreover, heightens the morale of the employees, for it helps in reducing dissatisfaction, complaints, grievances and absenteeism and reduces the rate of turn over. Further, trained employees make a better and economical use of materials and equipments; therefore, wastage and spoilage are lessened, and the need for the constant supervision is reduced. Trained employees would be a valuable asset to an organisation. Organizational objectives like viability, stability and growth can also be achieved through training. Jointly we can study it as:

- **Training Helps In Optimum Utilization Of Human Resources:** Training and Development helps in optimizing the utilization of human resource that further helps the employee to achieve the organizational goals as well as their individual goals.
- **Training Is Helpful In Development Of Human Resources:** Training and Development helps to provide an opportunity for the development of human resources' technical and behavioral skills in an organization. It also helps the employees in attaining personal growth.
- **Training Helps In Development Of Skills Of Employees:** Training and Development helps in increasing the job knowledge and skills of employees at each level. It helps to expand the horizons of human intellect and an overall personality of the employees.
- **Training Is Helpful In Increasing Productivity:** Training and Development helps in increasing the productivity of the employees that helps the organization further to achieve its long-term goals.
- **Training Promotes Team Spirit:** Training and Development helps in inculcating the sense of team work, team spirit, and inter-team collaborations. It helps in inculcating the zeal to learn within the employees.
- **Training And Development Is Helpful In Developing Organization's Culture:** Training and Development helps to develop and improve the organizational health, culture and effectiveness. It helps in creating the learning culture within the organization.
- **Training And Development Helps In Building The Organization's Climate:** Training and Development helps in building the positive perception and feelings about the organization. The employees get these feelings from leaders, subordinates, and peers.
- **Training Is Helpful In Improving The Quality:** Training and Development helps in improving upon the quality of work and work-life.
- **Training Helps In Creating Healthy Work Environment:** Training and Development helps in creating the healthy working environment. It helps to build good employee relationship so that individual goals align with organizational goals.
- **Training Helps In Improving The Health And Safety:** Training and Development helps in improving the health and safety of the organization thus preventing obsolescence.

- **Training Is Helpful In Improving Morale:** Training and Development helps in improving the morale of the work force.
- **Training Is Helpful In Creating A Better Corporate Image:** Training and Development helps in creating a better corporate image.
- **Training Leads To Improved Profitability:** Training and Development leads to improved profitabilit y and more positive attitudes towards profit orientation.
- **Training And Development Aids In Organizational Development** i.e. Organization gets more effective decision making and problem solving. It helps in understanding and carrying out organizational policies.
- **Training And Development Helps In Developing:** leadership skills, motivation, loyalty, better attitudes, and other aspects that successful workers and managers usually display.

Benefits of Training

The benefits of training can be segregated under following heads:

Training Benefits to the Organization

- Leads to improved profitability and/or more positive attitudes towards profits orientation.
- Improves the job knowledge and skills at all levels of the organization.
- Improves the morale of the workforce.
- Helps people identify with organizational goals.
- Helps create a better corporate image.
- Leads to authenticity, openness and trust.
- Improves the relationship between boss and subordinate.
- Aids in organizational development.
- Learns from the trainee.
- Helps prepare guidelines for work.
- Aids in understanding and carrying on organizational policies.
- Provides recognition for future needs in all areas of the organization.
- Organizations get more effective in decision-making and problem solving.
- Aids in development for promotion from within.
- Aids in developing leadership skill, motivation, loyalty, better attitudes, and other aspects that successful workers and managers usually display.
- Aids in increasing productivity and/ or quality of work.

- Helps keep costs down in many areas, for e.g. production, personnel, administration, etc.
- Develops a sense of responsibility to the organization for being competent and knowledgeable.
- Improves labour-management relations.
- Reduces outside consulting costs by utilizing competent internal consultants.
- Stimulates preventive management as opposed to putting out fires.
- Eliminates sub-optimal behavior (such as hiding tools).
- Creates an appropriate climate for growth and communication.
- Aids in improving organizational communication.
- Helps employees adjust to change.
- Aids in handling conflict, thereby helping to prevent stress and tension.

Benefits to the Individual

- Helps the individual in making better decisions and effective problem solving.
- Through training and development motivational variables of recognition, achievement, growth, responsibility and advancement are internalized and operationalised.
- Aids in encouraging and achieving self-development and self-confidence.
- Helps a person handle stress, tension, frustration and conflict
- Provides information for improving leadership knowledge, communication skills and attitudes.
- Increases job satisfaction and recognition.
- Moves a person towards personal goals while improving interactive skills.
- Satisfies, personal needs of the trainer and trainee.
- Provides the trainee an avenue for growth and a say in his/her own future.
- Develops a sense of growth and learning.
- Helps a person develop speaking and listening skills; also writing skills when exercises are required.
- Helps eliminate fear in attempting new tasks.

Benefits in Personnel and Human Relations

- Improves communication between groups and individuals.
- Aids in orientation for new employees and those taking new jobs through transfer or promotion.
- Provides information on equal opportunity and affirmative action.

- Provides information on other governmental laws and administrative policies.
- Improves interpersonal skills.
- Makes organizational policies, rules and regulations viable.
- Improves morale.
- Builds cohesiveness in groups.
- Provides a good climate for learning, growth and co-ordination.
- Makes the organization a better place to work and live.

TRAINING AND EDUCATION

	Training	**Education**
Definition	The process of affecting change in individual human's behavior often applied to the acquisition of limited operating job related skills.	Learning or acquiring orderly, logical systems for processing new information.
Purpose	Supplies the specific skill, knowledge, or attitudes needed to meet the goals of organization (usually performing assigned task within specific productivity standards)	Provides knowledge, skills and values needed for successful living with the culture, plus the ability to deal effectively with new data and changing conditions.
Scope	Deals with specific tasks related to job performance.	Deals with a complex set of attitudes, skills, and values.
Time-frame	Deals with current needs and immediate application; short-term orientation normal.	Long-term orientations, dealing with future application of current learning.
Responsibility	Leadership at all levels of the organization; special burdens on all types of training specialists.	Leadership of nation agency sector, or enterprise, special burdens rest on manpower planners; state and national planning.
Expected outcome	A human (or group of humans) who can perform a specific task to specified standards in order to meet predetermined goals.	A human (or group of humans) who continuously acquires and effectively processes new information-education shapes and moulds attitudes.

Development

INTRODUCTION

Development refers to those learning opportunities designed to help employees grow. Development is not primarily skill oriented. Instead, it provides general knowledge and attitudes which will be helpful to employees in higher positions. Efforts towards development often depend on personal drive and ambition. Development activities, such as those supplied by management development programmes, are generally voluntary.

Development is a related process. It covers not only those activities which improve job performance but also those which bring about growth of the personality; which helps individuals in the progress towards maturity and actualization of their potential capacities so that they become not only good employees but better men and women. Training a person for bigger and higher job is development. And this may well include not only imparting specific skills and knowledge but also inculcating certain personality and mental attitudes.

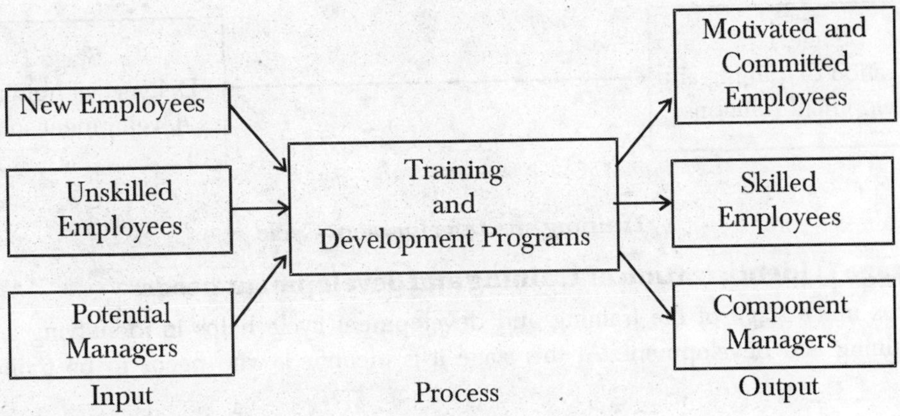

Employee training is distinct from management development or executive development programmes. While the former refers to training given to employees in the areas of operation, technical and allied areas, the latter refers to developing an employee in the areas of principles and techniques of management, administration, organization, and allied areas.

Distinction Between Training and Development

Area	***Training***	***Development***
Content	Technical skills and knowledge	Managerial and behavioral skills and knowledge
Purpose	Specific job-related	Conceptual and general knowledge
Duration	Short-term	Long-term
For whom	Mostly technical and non managerial Personnel	Mostly for managerial Personnel

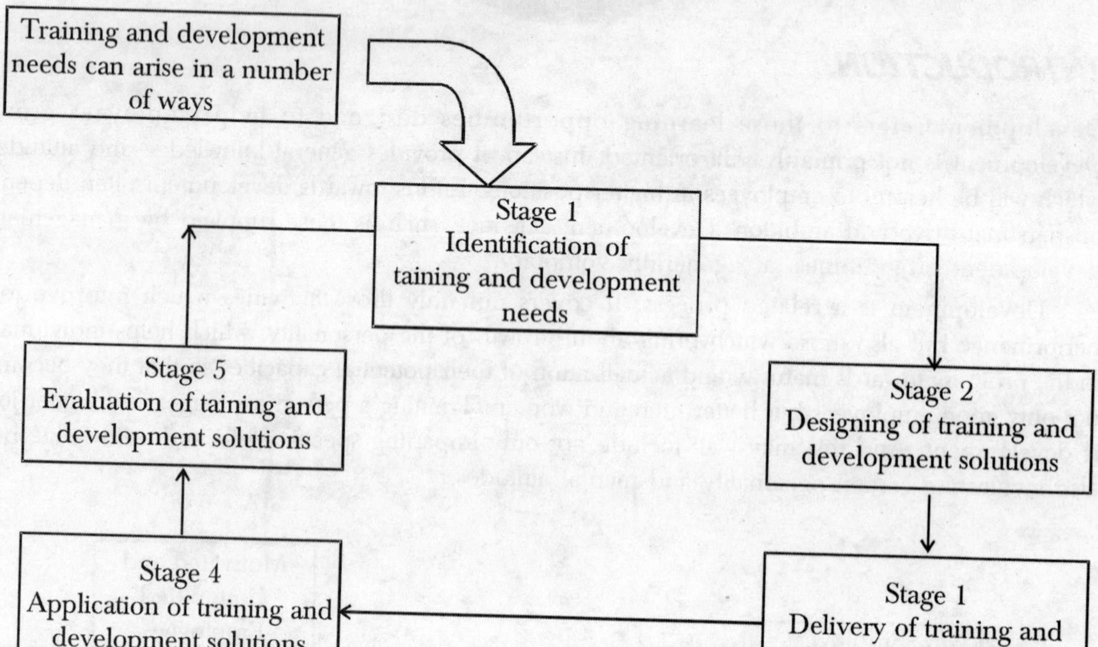

Training and Development Cycle

Stage 1: Identification of training and development needs:

This initial stage of the training and development cycle helps in identifying a need for training and development. At this stage it is identified, who needs to be trained, when and how the training should be conducted so as to improve the performance and achieve success.

Stage 2: Designing of training and development solutions:

This stage covers planning, design and development of training. It aims to ensure that a systematic and consistent approach is adopted for all training and development solutions. Training and development solutions cover face to face training, open and flexible learning including e-learning.

Stage 3: Delivery of training and development solutions:

This stage of the training and development cycle ensures that the delivery of the training is effective and provides opportunities for the learners to learn. This will involve choosing the most appropriate format for meeting training and development needs, and taking advantage of different training and development methods.

Stage 4: Application of training and development solutions:

This stage of the training and development cycle is concerned with ensuring that all learning outcomes are applied and reinforced. This stage will help those who monitor the development of individual learners and review their progress.

Stage 5: Evaluation of training and development solutions:

This stage of the training and development cycle deals with the collection, analysis and presentation of information to establish the improvement in performance resulted after the training. This stage will help those who evaluate learning programmes, or who respond to developments in learning, or plan and introduce improvements in learning interventions.

Systems Approach to Training

Training is a sub-system of the organization because the departments such as, marketing & sales, HR, production, finance, etc depends on training for its survival. Training is a transforming process that requires some input and in turn it produces output in the form of knowledge, skills, and attitudes (KSAs).

The Training System

A System is a combination of things or parts that must work together to perform a particular function. An organization is a system and training is a sub system of the organization.

The System Approach views training as a sub system of an organization. System Approach can be used to examine broad issues like objectives, functions, and aims of training programmes. It establishes a logical relationship between the sequential stages in the process of training need analysis (TNA), formulating, delivering, and evaluating training programmes.

There are 4 necessary inputs i.e. technology, man, material, time required in every system to produce products or services. And every system must have some output from these inputs in order to survive. The output can be tangible or intangible depending upon the organization's requirement. A system approach to training is planned creation of training program. This approach uses step-by-step procedures to solve the problems. Under systematic approach, training is undertaken on planned basis. Out of this planned effort, one such basic model of five steps is system model that is explained below.

Organizations are working in open environment i.e. there are some internal and external forces, that poses threats and opportunities, therefore, trainers need to be aware of these forces which may impact on the content, form, and conduct of the training efforts. The internal forces are the various demands of the organization for a better learning environment; needs to be up to dated with the latest technologies.

The three models of training are:

1. System Model
2. Transitional Model
3. Instructional System Development Model

SYSTEMATIC MODEL TRAINING

The system model consists of five phases and should be repeated on a regular basis to make further improvements. The training should achieve the purpose of helping employees to perform their work to required standards. The steps involved in System Model of training are as follows:

1. **Analyze and identify the training needs:** Which is to analyze the department, job, employees' requirement, who needs training, what do they need to learn, estimating training cost, etc. The next step is to develop a performance measure on the basis of which actual performance would be evaluated.
2. **Design and provide training to meet identified needs:** This step requires developing objectives of training, identifying the learning steps, sequencing and structuring the contents.

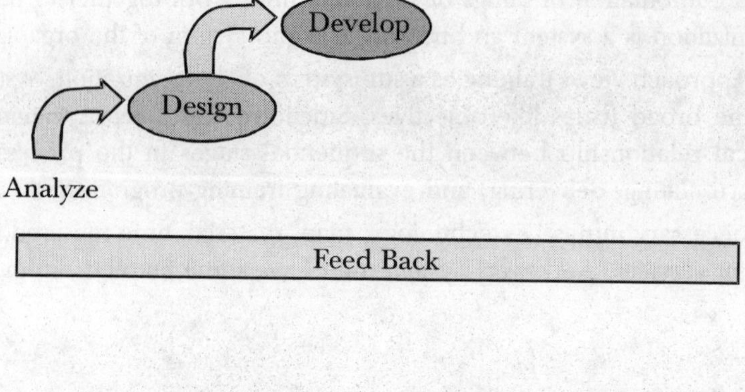

3. **Develop:** This phase requires listing the activities in the training program that will assist the participants to learn, selecting delivery method, examining the training material, validating information to be imparted to make sure it accomplishes all the goals & objectives.
4. **Implementing:** is the hardest part of the system because one wrong step can lead to the failure of whole training program.
5. **Evaluating:** evaluating each phase so as to make sure it has achieved its aim in terms of subsequent work performance. Making necessary amendments to any of the previous stages in order to remedy or improve failure practices.

Transitional Model: Transitional model focuses on the organization as a whole. The outer loop describes the vision, mission and values of the organization on the basis of which training model i.e. inner loop is executed.

- **Vision:** focuses on the milestones that the organization would like to achieve after the defined point of time. A vision statement tells that where the organization sees itself few years down the line. A vision may include setting a role mode, or bringing some internal transformation, or may be promising to meet some other deadlines.
- **Mission:** explains the reason of organizational existence. It identifies the position in the community. The reason of developing a mission statement is to motivate, inspire, and inform the employees regarding the organization. The mission statement tells about the identity that how the organization would like to be viewed by the customers, employees, and all other stakeholders.
- **Values:** is the translation of vision and mission into communicable ideals. It reflects the deeply held values of the organization and is independent of current industry environment. For example, values may include social responsibility, excellent customer service, etc.

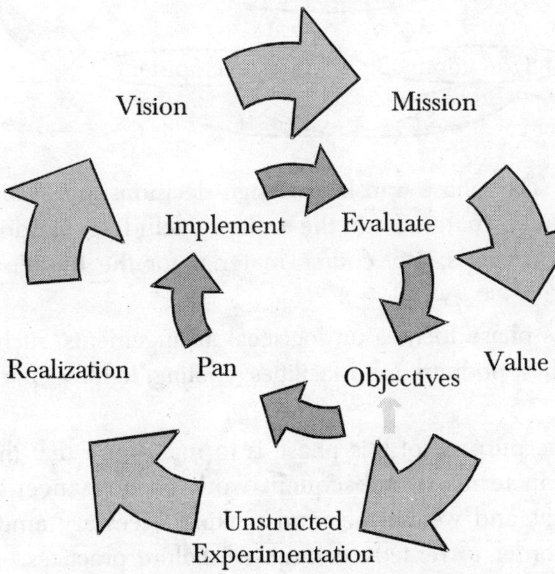

The mission, vision, and values precede the objective in the inner loop. This model considers the organization as a whole. The objective is formulated keeping these three things in mind and then the training model is further implemented.

Instructional System Development Model (ISD) Model: Instructional System Development model or ISD training model was made to answer the training problems. This model is widely used now-a-days in the organization because it is concerned with the training need on the job performance. Training objectives are defined on the basis of job responsibilities and job description and on the basis of the defined objectives, individual progress is measured. This model also helps in determining and developing the favorable strategies, sequencing the content, and delivering media for the types of training objectives to be achieved.

The Instructional System Development model comprises of five stages:

1. **Analysis:** This phase consist of training need assessment, job analysis, and target audience analysis.
2. **Planning:** This phase consist of setting goal of the learning outcome, instructional objectives that measures behavior of a participant after the training, types of training material, media selection, methods of evaluating the trainee, trainer and the training program, strategies to impart knowledge i.e. selection of content, sequencing of content, etc.

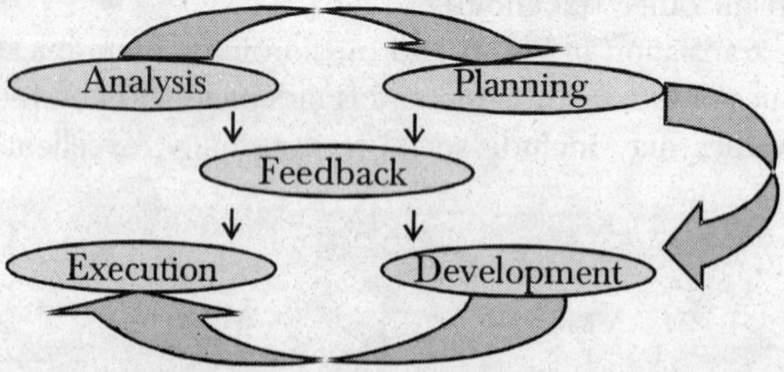

3. **Development:** This phase translates design decisions into training material. It consists of developing course material for the trainer including handouts, workbooks, visual aids, demonstration props, etc, course material for the trainee including handouts of summary.
4. **Execution:** This phase focuses on logistical arrangements, such as arranging speakers, equipments, benches, podium, food facilities, cooling, lighting, parking, and other training accessories.
5. **Evaluation:** The purpose of this phase is to make sure that the training program has achieved its aim in terms of subsequent work performance. This phase consists of identifying strengths and weaknesses and making necessary amendments to any of the previous stage in order to remedy or improve failure practices.

The ISD model is a continuous process that lasts throughout the training program. It also highlights that feedback is an important phase throughout the entire training program. In this model, the output of one phase is an input to the next phase.

Case Study

HINDUSTAN AERONAUTICS LTD.

Vision: 'To make HAL a dynamic, vibrant, value based learning oragnisation with Human Resources exceptionally skilled, highly motivated and committed to meet the current and future challenges. This will be driven by core values of the company fully embedded in the culture of the organisation.'

Training and Development

Training is one of the most important interventions for developing human resources. Hence, identification of training competency profile in terms of the vision and mission of the company would help in formulating a training and development strategy for the company. The following objectives have been set in this regards:

- To provide training to all employees at regular interval in a plan period of 5 years
- To make training an integral component of individual professional evolution
- Updating knowledge to avoid obsolescence
- Enhancing professional creativity
- Enabling employees to shoulder higher responsibility
- To create a business bias and strategic thinking to take up new business challenges (creation of a centre of excellence, etc.)

The goals of training will be progressively achieved by seven days training per employee per year with a budget of 2% of annual wage bill. Keeping in view the organisational requirements and the above goals and objectives of training, the following has been identified as the key focus area of training:

- Technology
- Tooling
- Quality
- Information technology

Furthermore, to facilitate development of soft skills (change of mind set, managerial development) training would be imparted on continuous basis. Tie-ups with centers of excellence, such as IITs, NDC, and FIAS, France, for training would be given prime importance.

Scheme for Learning and Certification of Executives: An organisation has to be a 'learning organisation' for survival in the present era of liberalization, privatization, and globalization. Therefore, 'knowledge' is the only core competence of organisations for coping with changes.

Since individual knowledge is the starting point for organisational knowledge, only the employees can convert knowledge into efficient action. In line with the above philosophy among other initiatives like institutionalizing learning centers in divisions, etc., HAL has also introduced the scheme for Learning and Certification for executives as a starting point for individual knowledge. The scheme inter alia provides opportunity for the junior and middle management cadre executives to broaden their perspectives by learning not only about all functions and procedures in their respective discipline but also about related areas, the overall organisation, and its environment. So far, approximately 45% (both for 'O' and 'A' level) of executives have been certified. It is proposed to expand the coverage of this team further, if required, by linking it to some kind of reward mechanism. Lastly, the HRD plan will also include time-to-time OD interventions to address specific requirements of the company.

Q. Is training important?

Summary

This chapter begins with an introduction to the contemporary competitive scenario and explains the definitions, principles importance of training. It also explains the importance of training and the benefits of training to the individual and the organization. It also gives introduction to development and the training and development cycle. It further explains the differences between training and development, training and education, it also explains the systems approach to training and its three models; System Model, Instructional System Development Model and Transitional model of training.

Concept Review Questions

OBJECTIVES

1. Every organisation needs to have well _______ and _______ people to perform the activities that have to be done.
2. Training is a process of _______ a sequence of programmed behaviors.
3. Management should take care to _______ the successful trainees.
4. Training is the corner stone of sound management for it makes employees more _______ and _______.
5. Training and Development helps in building the positive _______ and feelings about the organization.
6. Training and Development leads to improved _______ and more positive attitudes towards profit orientation.
7. Development is not primarily _______ oriented.

8. Efforts towards development often depend on personal drive and _______.
   (trained /experienced, learning, reward, effective/ productive, perception, profitability, skill, ambition)

SHORT QUESTIONS

1. Define training.
2. Mention any two principles of training.
3. Mention any two differences between education and training.
4. Explain the term development.
5. Mention any two differences between training and development.
6. What are the components of the training and development cycle?
7. What do you mean by systems approach to training?
8. What are the benefits of training to the organizations?
9. In what ways training is helpful to the individuals?
10. Write a short-note on:
    (*a*) Importance of training.
    (*b*) Instructional System Development Model
    (*c*) Reddy's acronym of training
    (*d*) Training system

LONG QUESTIONS

1. Define the term training and development and elaborate their differences.
2. Explain the importance of training and development.
3. What are the important principles of training?
4. How is training beneficial to the organizations, individuals and human relations?
5. What do you mean by systematic model training? Explain its steps.
6. What do mean the transitional model of training? And what are its components?
7. Explain the Instructional System Development Model (ISD) Model. And what are its five stages?
8. Explain in detail the difference between training and education.
9. "Training and Development are two sides of the same coin" comment.
10. How is training different from development? Explain.

2

Psychology of Learning

PSYCHOLOGY OF LEARNING AND LEARNED MOTIVATION

Learning is the process of encoding, retaining, and using information. Learning depends on participation and repetition. It is quick and long lasting when the learner participates actively. Participation and involvement improves motivation and engages more senses, which reinforce the learning process. Repetition of message builds a pattern into one's memory. Learning principles are guidelines to the ways in which people learn most effectively. In a training programme, the effectiveness of learning depends on a body of predefined knowledge or skills, expressed in terms of measurable objectives that are often behavioral in nature. Having studied the basics of learning, you now need to be acquainted with the laws of learning.

Laws of Learning

The laws of learning are as follows:

- **Law of Intensity:** Learning depends on the strength of the response to the stimulus condition.
- **Law of Organization:** Learning is more rapid when materials are organized into meaningful relationships.
- **Law of Continuity:** This law refers to closeness and intimacy established between the teachers and the trainees. All events associated, directly or indirectly with the training must be completed within the specific time limit.
- **Law of Exercise:** Performance of an act tends to make subsequent performance of the act easier.
- **Law of Effect:** Response leading to a satisfying result is likely to be learned.

These five laws prompt to strengthen the stimulus, giving organized materials relevant to the work situations, establishing closeness and intimacy with the trainees within the time frame of the training period and help trainees to perform smoothly and get positive responses.

Principles of Learning

Learning principles are guidelines to the ways in which people learn most effectively. The principles of learning are as follows:

- **Principle of Readiness:** The most important work is to make the trainees ready to learn. This readiness can be created by letting the learners know the importance of training for performing their tasks more easily and faster, for accomplishing the work without any defect. They can further be convinced by highlighting the benefits such as performance linked pay and incentives. This will enhance their willingness to learn.
- **Principle of Association:** The learners must be encouraged to broaden their known horizon. In other words, they must get support to move from the known horizon to the unknown horizon. But the curriculum should be such that they can move from the known to the unknown in small steps; start with simple steps and gradually build up to the new and more difficult task.
- **Principle of Involvement:** For significant learning to occur the learners must be actively involved in the learning process. A good instructor uses learners involvement tools, such as, questions and answers, group discussions, audiovisual aids, case problems, role playing, simulations, quizzes, and application exercises. This should be done by the programme coordinator as the lack of involvement leads to little or no learning.
- **Principle of Repetition:** The trainees must get the opportunity of applying the knowledge disseminated by the trainers. Repetition helps learning, retention, recall and helps in administering the exercises covering the topics taught so that the trainees can readily apply the knowledge gained in the lecture session. This will embed the knowledge or skills, help them to retain, and recall the knowledge in the work area.

Learning concepts and theories are based on firmly rooted and well-grounded educational and psychological principles, which can further be elaborated as the following:

1. Every human being is capable of learning. Each has an intellectual capacity and the ability to learn from training.
2. It is easier for the trainee to understand/remember material that is meaningful. Training materials may be made more meaningful at least in six ways:
   (*a*) At the start of training, the trainee should be provided with the birds' eye view of the material to be presented. Knowing the overall picture and understanding how each part of the programme fits into it helps make the entire programme meaningful.
   (*b*) When presenting material to the trainees, a variety of similar examples should be used.
   (*c*) The training material is organized in a logical manner and has meaningful units.
   (*d*) The material should be split up into meaningful chunks rather than presenting it all at once.
   (*e*) The terms and concepts that are already familiar to the trainees should be used.
   (*f*) As many visual aids should be used as possible to augment "theoretical" material.

3. The training programme should be planned in a logical manner so that each succeeding step builds upon the previous one–the probability of success increases because the trainee encounters the steps in sequence. The best course for changing behaviour is to bring about the transition through a progression of small, orderly steps.
4. A new employee may learn in order to please his boss, to get confirmed in his job, to acquire the requisite knowledge and skills to perform it in a much better and more effective manner. Supervisors may go in for training to learn how to delegate responsibility more effectively, how to save their own limited time, how to read reports quickly, how to understand their subordinates better, how to eliminate potential labour troubles, and how to administer the agreements reached between employees and the management.
5. Different levels of learning exist. Learning may involve awareness, changed attitudes and changed behaviour. It may involve mental processes or physical strength. Different time and method requirements are needed to bring about different levels of learning.
6. The basic principles of training design consist of:
   (*a*) Identifying the components of tasks of final desired performance,
   (*b*) Assuring that each component is fully achieved and,
   (*c*) Arranging the total learning situation in a sequence.
7. Learning objectives should be stabilized for every training programme. These objectives guide the instructor in planning the training, guide the trainee, and provide criteria for evaluating how much learning has been achieved. A complete statement of learning objectives clearly specifies the behaviour expected of the trainee after the instruction has taken place, the condition under which the trainee will be required to demonstrate the prescribed behaviour, and the standard of acceptable performance. Knowledge of standards of performance makes learning effective and the goals and benchmarks enable the learner to judge his educational achievements and process.
8. An adequate interest in, and motivation for, learning are essential because people are goal-oriented. They work to satisfy their needs for self-expression, self-accomplishment, self-actualization, and financial incentives. However, most learning is self-motivated and related to the attainment of personal goals. The trainer must explain to the trainee how his training can be instrumental in his success. Trainer should first clarify the goals of the training; then explain how job performance is related to reward; and explain how the training will improve his performance and thereby boost his reward.
9. Learning is active and not passive. Effective education costs for action and active involvement on the part of all participants. Researchers have revealed (in America) that people remember 10% of what they read, 20% of what they hear, 30% of what they see, 50% of what they see and hear, 70% of what they say, 90% of what they say as they perform the task. In other words, people learn best and more by doing than by hearing. The larger number of human senses involved, the better the training.

Different training methods are used for different types of learning. For e.g., cognitive learning stresses audio and visual experience to gain understanding. It may involve reading, lectures, audio-visual presentation, case problem, examination, etc. Effective learning (i.e., attitude, value, and interest acquisitions) may best be learned through field-trips, role playing, open ended discussion, counseling or reflection. Psychomotor learning (doing skills) can be acquired best through practice, drill, behaviour modifications, simulation games, demonstrations, internships, etc. Therefore, the value of multi-sensory leaning exercises should be emphasized.

10. Previous experience of the individual trainee affects his learning experiences. New material is related to his previous knowledge. New behaviour is formulated using existing foundations as a basis.
11. People learn more and even faster when they are told of their achievements, that is, they should have Knowledge of Results (KR) or feedback. Such feed back should be specific rather than general. It should be precise and diagnostic rather than evaluative. It should be directed at the behaviour so that the learner can do something right and develop individual personality traits.

    It should be the automatic, immediate and meaningfully related to work that is done. In-the-job-training, an employee should be informed of his success or failure so that he may adjust his efforts, if necessary or correct his mistakes. The trainer should not wait until the end of the day to tell a trainee that "he has done well". Instead, reinforcement should be frequent, whenever he does something right.
12. Training in one activity that can be transferred to another if, there are similar components and principles. Once a general principle has been learned, all problems of similar nature can be solved as they arise. For e.g., a manager trained in the techniques of contingency leadership theory may be capable of analyzing a wide variety of motivational problems and developing solutions to them on the basis of his knowledge for a few basic principle.

    Transfer of training can be accomplished by:

    (*a*) Maximizing the similarity between the training situation and the work situation.

    (*b*) Providing adequate experience with tasks during training.

    (*c*) Providing for a variety of examples while teaching concepts or skills.

    (*d*) Identifying important features of the task.

    (*e*) Making sure that the trainee understands general principles.
13. The training that involves understanding complex problems and discovering new alternative solutions can be achieved best when the environment is relaxed and free of anxiety and the trainees are not under any immediate pressure to produce.
14. Difference in abilities, backgrounds, experiences, readiness to learn and other factors cause individual trainees who acquire new knowledge, skills, and attitudes at differing rates of speed. Training programmes necessarily must be adapted to the training speeds of the separate trainees.

15. Time must be provided to practice what has been learned. The learning process requires a great deal of time for assimilation, testing, acceptance, and the development of confidence. Repetition, accompanied by constant efforts towards improvement, makes for an effective development of skills. Practice makes a man perfect. Moreover, skills that are practiced often are better learned and not forgotten easily.
16. Learning is closely related to attention and concentration. The learning process is more effective if distractions are avoided.
17. Learning is more effective when one shares one's -knowledge, prejudice, bias, likes and dislikes, that is, when one abandons the "I know attitude" and adopts the "I want to know" approach.
18. Early success increases an individual's chances for effective learning, for "nothing succeeds like success".
19. Trainers are important ingredient in the learning environment. They should know the material, to be able to communicate, and be aware of the learner's needs. The old saying, "If the student failed to learn, the teacher failed to teach", contains a great deal of truth.

LEARNING PATTERNS

Trainers need some understanding of the patterns in which new skills are learned. The employee is likely to find himself unusually clumsy during the early stages of learning. This can be called discouraging stage. After the employee adjusts himself to the environment, he learns at a faster rate. A 'plateau' develops after the lapse of more training time due to a loss of motivation and lack of break in training schedule and time. The trainee reaches the next stage when he is motivated by the trainer and/are some break or pause in time and training process. The trainee at this stage learns at a fast rate.

Characteristics of Learning Process: The characteristics of learning process are as follows:

1. Learning is a continuous process.
2. People learn through their actual personal experience, simulated experience and from other's experience (by using the knowledge which represents experience of others).
3. People learn step by step, from known to unknown and simple to complex.
4. There is a need for repetition in teaching to improve skill and to learn perfectly.
5. Practice makes a man perfect. Hence, opportunity should be created to use and transfer the skills, knowledge and ability acquired through learning. It gives satisfaction to the learner.
6. Conflicts in learning: Conflict in learning arises when the trainer knows or has developed some habits which are incorrect in the term of the method being learned.

Climate for Learning

Conducive climate is highly essential for serious participation, attentiveness, creation of interest and sincerity of learner. Climate for learning consists of working conditions, relationship with other trainees, and trainers/instructors, conditions for relaxation, freedom, scope for social interaction, and formation of social groups.

Conducive climate for learning should be provided in view of its significance in training. It consists of ideal physical and physiological environment. Ideal physical environment, consisting of suitable location with space, adequate accommodation, audio-visual aids, air conditioning, ventilation, lighting and other facilities like canteen, facilities for relaxation, should be provided. Ideal physiological environment, consisting business atmosphere, friendly environment, frequent communication, follow-up regarding performance and progress, enthusiastic, helpful an broadminded trainer etc, should be created and provided. Provision for measuring learner's progress through tests should also be made in order to regulate, correct and follow-up the training programmes.

LEARNED MOTIVATION

To understand how individual differences affect the learning process, there are many different theories of how people learn. What follows is a variety of them, and it is useful to consider their application to how the employees learn and also how they are taught during the training programmes.

Burns (1995) 'conceives of learning as a relatively permanent change in behaviour with behaviour including both observable activity and internal processes such as thinking, attitudes and emotions.' It is clear that **Burns** includes motivation in this definition of learning. Burns considers that learning might not manifest itself in observable behaviour until some time after the training program has taken place.

Theories of Learning

- Sensory stimulation theory
- Reinforcement theory
- Cognitive-Gestalt approaches
- Holistic learning theory
- Facilitation theory
- Experiential learning
- Action learning
- Adult learning (Andragogy)

• Sensory Stimulation Theory

Traditional sensory stimulation theory has as its basic premise that effective learning occurs when the senses are stimulated (**Laird**, 1985). Laird quotes research that found that the vast majority of knowledge held by adults (75%) is learned through seeing. Hearing is the next most effective (about 13%) and the other senses - touch, smell and taste account for 12% of what we know. By stimulating the senses, especially the visual sense, learning can be enhanced. However, this theory says that if multi-senses are stimulated, greater learning takes place. Stimulation through the senses is achieved through a greater variety of colors, volume levels, strong statements, facts presented visually, use of a variety of techniques and media.

• Reinforcement Theory

This theory was developed by the behaviorist school of psychology, notably by **B.F. Skinner** earlier this century. Skinner believed that behaviour is a function of its consequences. The learner will repeat the desired behaviour if positive reinforcement (a pleasant consequence) follows the behaviour.

Positive reinforcement, or 'rewards' can include verbal reinforcement such as 'That's great' or 'You're certainly on the right track' through to more tangible rewards such as a certificate at the end of the course or promotion to a higher level in an organisation.

Negative reinforcement also strengthens behaviour and refers to a situation when a negative condition is stopped or avoided as a consequence of the behaviors. Punishment, on the other hand, weakens behaviour because a negative condition is introduced or experienced as a consequence of the behaviour and teaches the individual not to repeat the behaviour which was negatively reinforced. A set of conditions is created which are designed to eliminate behavior. This aspect of behaviorism has little or no relevance to education. However, punishment is widely used in everyday life although it only works for a short time and often only when the punishing agency is present.

Competency Based Training is based on this theory, and although it is useful in learning repetitive tasks like multiplication tables and those work skills that require a great deal of practice, higher order learning is not involved. There is criticism of this approach that it is rigid and mechanical.

• Cognitive-Gestalt approaches

The emphasis here is on the importance of experience, meaning, problem-solving and the development of insights. This theory has developed the concept that individuals have different needs and concerns at different times, and that they have subjective interpretations in different contexts.

• Holistic Learning Theory

The basic premise of this theory is that the 'individual personality consists of many elements specifically the intellect, emotions, the body impulse (or desire), intuition and imagination, that all require activation if learning is to be more effective.

• Facilitation Theory (The Humanist Approach)

Carl Rogers and others have developed the theory of facilitative learning. The basic premise of this theory is that learning will occur by the educator acting as a facilitator, that is by establishing an atmosphere in which learners feel comfortable to consider new ideas and are not threatened by external factors.

Other characteristics of this theory include:

- A belief that human beings have a natural eagerness to learn,
- There is some resistance to, and unpleasant consequences of, giving up what is currently held to be true,
- The most significant learning involves changing one's concept of oneself.

Facilitative teachers are:

- Less protective of their constructs and beliefs than other teachers,
- More able to listen to learners, especially to their feelings,
- Inclined to pay as much attention to their relationship with learners as to the content of the course,
- Apt to accept feedback, both positive and negative and to use it as constructive insight into themselves and their behaviour.

Learners:

- Are encouraged to take responsibility for their own learning,
- Provide much of the input for the learning which occurs through their insights and experiences,
- Are encouraged to consider that the most valuable evaluation is self-evaluation and that learning needs to focus on factors that contribute to solving significant problems or achieving significant results.

• Experiential Learning

Kolb proposed a four-stage learning process with a model that is often referred to in describing experiential learning. The process can begin at any of the stages and is continuous, i.e. there is no limit to the number of cycles you can make in a learning situation. This theory asserts that without reflection we would simply continue to repeat our mistakes.

Honey and Mumford identified four learning styles:

- Activist (enjoys the experience itself),

- Reflector (spends a great deal of time and effort reflecting)
- Theorist (good at making connections and abstracting ideas from experience)
- Pragmatist (enjoys the planning stage)

There are strengths and weaknesses in each of these styles. **Honey and Mumford** argue that learning is enhanced when we think about our learning style so that we can build on strengths and work towards minimizing weaknesses to improve the quality of learning.

• *Action Learning*

Action Learning is the approach that links the world of learning with the world of action through a reflective process within small cooperative learning groups known as 'action learning sets'. The 'sets' meet regularly to work on individual members' real-life issues with the aim of learning with and from each other. The 'father' of Action Learning, **Reg Revans**, has said that there can be no learning without action and no (sober and deliberate) action without learning.

Revans argued that learning can be shown by the following equation, where L is learning; P is programmed knowledge (e.g. traditional instruction) and Q is questioning insight.

$$L = P + Q$$

Revans, along with many others who have used, researched and taught about this approach, argued that Action Learning is ideal for finding solutions to problems that do not have a 'right' answer because the necessary questioning insight can be facilitated by people learning with and from each other in action learning 'sets'.

• *Adult Learning (Andragogy)*

Malcolm Knowles is the theorist who brought the concept of adult learning to the fore. He has argued that adulthood has arrived when people behave in adult ways and believe themselves to be adults. Then they should be treated as adults. He taught that adult learning was special in a number of ways. For example:

- Adult learners bring a great deal of experience to the learning environment. Educators can use this as a resource.
- Adults expect to have a high degree of influence on what they are to be educated for, and how they are to be educated.
- The active participation of learners should be encouraged in designing and implementing educational programs.
- Adults need to be able to see applications for new learning.
- Adult learners expect to have a high degree of influence on how learning will be evaluated.
- Adults expect their responses to be acted upon when asked for feedback on the progress of the program.
- By adulthood people are self-directing. This is the concept that lies at the heart of andragogy... andragogy is therefore, experience-based, problem-oriented and collaborative

very much in the spirit of the humanist approach to learning and education ... the whole educational activity turns on the student.

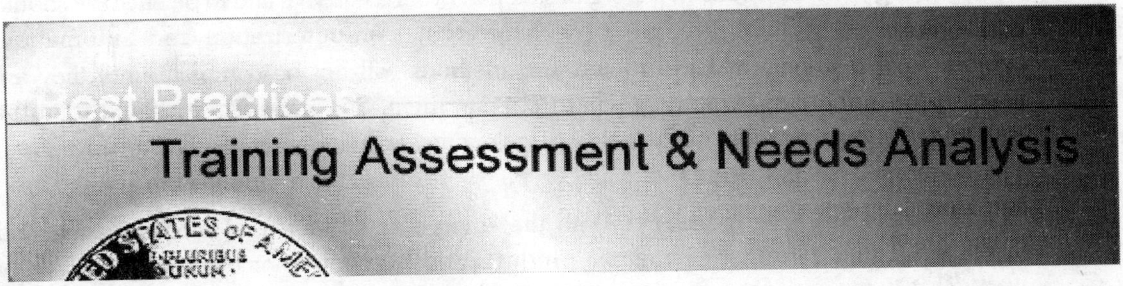

NEED FOR TRAINING

Every organisation big or small, productive or non-productive, economic or social, old or newly established should provide training to all employees irrespective of their qualification, skill, and suitability for the job. Thus, no organisation can choose whether or not to train employees.

Training is not something that is done once to new employees; it is used continuously in every well run establishment. Further, technological changes and automation require up-dating the skills and knowledge. As such an organisation has to retain the old employees.

Specifically, the need for training arises due to the following reasons:

1. **To Match the Employee Specifications with the Job Requirements and Organizational Needs:** An employee's specification may not exactly suit to the requirement of the job and the organisation irrespective of his past experience, qualifications, skills, knowledge etc. Thus, every management finds deviations between employee's present specification and the job requirements and organizational needs. Training is needed to fill these gaps by developing and moulding the employee's skill, knowledge, attitude, behaviour etc. to match with the job requirements and organizational needs.
2. **Organisational Viability and the Transformation Process:** The primary goal of most of the organisations is their viability is continuously influenced by environmental pressure. If the organisation does not adapt itself to the changing factors in the environment, it will loose its market share. If the organisation desires to adapt these changes, first it has to train the employees to impart specific skills and knowledge in order to enable them to contribute to the organizational efficiency and to cope with the changing environment. In addition, it provides continuity to the organisation process and development. The productivity of the organisation can be improved by developing the efficiency of transformation process which in turn depends on enhancements of the existing level of skills and knowledge of the employees. The achievement of these objective

mostly depend on the effectiveness of the human resource that an organisation posses. Employee effectiveness can be secured by proper training.

3. **Technology Advances:** Every organisation in order to survive and to be effective should adopt the latest technology that is mechanization, computerization and automation. Adoption of latest technological means and methods will not be complete until they are manned by employees possessing skill to operate them. So, organisation should train the employees to enrich them in the areas of changing technical skills and knowledge from time to time.

4. **Organisational Complexity:** With the emergence of increased mechanization and automation, manufacturing of multiple products and bi-products or dealing in services of diversified lines, extension of operations to various regions of the country. In Overseas countries, organisation of most of the companies has become complex. This leads to growth in number and kind of employees and lawyers in organizational hierarchy. This creates the complex problems of co-ordination, integration and adaptability to the requirements of growth, diversification and expansion. Companies constantly search for opportunities to improve organizational effectiveness. Training is responsible for much of the planned change and effectiveness in an organisation as it prepares the people to be the change agents and to implement the programmes of effectiveness. Thus, training solves the problem of organizational complexity.

5. **Human Relations:** Trends in approach towards personal management have changed from the commodity approach to partnership approach, crossing the human relation approach. So today, managements of most of the organizations has to maintain human relations besides maintaining sound industrial relations although hitherto the managers are not accustomed to deal with the workers accordingly. So training in human relations is necessary to deal with human problems (including alienation, inter-personal and inter-group conflicts etc.) and to maintain human relations.

6. **Change in the Job Assignment:** Training is also necessary when the existing employee is promoted to the higher level in the organisation and when there is some new job or occupation due to transfer. Training is also necessary to equip the old employee with the advanced disciplines, techniques or technology.

The need for the training of employees can further be expressed by the observation made by the different authorities.

I. **To increase productivity:** "Instruction can help employees increase their level of performance on their present assignment. Increased human performance often directly leads to increase operational productivity and increased company profits." Again, "increased performance and productivity, because of training, are most evident on the part of new employees who are not yet fully aware of most efficient and effective ways of performing their jobs."

II. To improve quality: "Better informed workers are less likely to make operational mistakes. Quality increases may be in relationship to a company product or service, or in reference to the intangible organisation employment atmosphere."

III. To Help A Company Fulfill its Future Personnel Needs: "Organizations that have a good internal education programme will have to make less drastic manpower changes and adjustments in the event of sudden personnel alternations. When the need arises, organizational vacancies can more easily be staffed from internal sources if a company initiates and maintains an adequate instructional programme for both its non-supervisory and managerial employees.

IV. To Improve Organizational Climate: "An endless chain of positive reactions results from a well-planned training programme. Production and product quality may improve; financial incentives may then be increased, inter promotion become stressed, less supervisory pressure ensured and base pay rate increases results. Increased moral may be due to many factors, but one of the most important of these is the current state of an organisation's education and endeavor."

V. To Improve Health and Safety: "Proper training can help prevent industrial accidents. A safer work environment leads to more stable mental attitudes on the part of the employees. Managerial mental state would also improve if supervisors know that they can better themselves through company-designed development programmes."

VI. Obsolescence Prevention: "Training and development programmes foster the initiative and creativity of employees and help to prevent manpower obsolescence, which may be due to age, temperament or motivation, or the inability of a person to adapt himself to technological changes."

VII. Personal Growth: "Employees on a personal basis gain individually from their exposure to educational experiences." Again, "management development programmes seem to give participants a wider awareness, an enlarged skill, and enlightened altruistic philosophy, and make enhanced personal growth possible."

It may be observed that the need for training arises from more than one reason:

(*a*) An increased use of technology in production.

(*b*) Labour turnover arising from normal separation due to death or physical incapacity, for accidents, disease, superannuation, voluntary retirement, promotion within the organisation and change of occupation or job.

(*c*) Need for additional hands to cope with an increased production of goods and services;

(*d*) Employment of inexperienced and new labour requires detailed instruction for an effective performance of a job.

(*e*) Old employees need refresher training to enable them to keep abreast of the changing methods, techniques and use of sophisticated tools and equipments

(*f*) Need for enabling employees to do the work in a more effective way to reduce learning time, reduce supervision time, reduce waste and spoilage of raw material and produce quality goods and develop their potentials.

(*g*) Need or reducing grievances and minimizing accident rates
(*h*) Need for maintaining the validity of an organisation as a whole and raising morale of its employees.

Assessment of Training Needs

A training programme should be established only when it is felt that it would assist in the solution of specific operational problems. The first step in this process is, to make a thorough analysis of the entire organization, its operations and manpower resources available in order to find out 'The trouble spots' where training may be needed.

It should, however, be noted that training is not a cure for all. For example, if the efficiency of an employee is low, or he cannot get the job done, it may be due to faulty raw materials and equipment or not getting their timely supplies, or a defective engineering design, or uncongenial environment, or low wages, or tax supervision. If that is the case, these problems should be rectified.

Identification Of Training Needs Must Contain Three Types Of Analysis:

1. **Organizational Analysis:** It involves a study of the entire organization in terms of objectives, its resources, resource allocation and utilization, growth potential and its environment. Its purpose is to determine where training emphasis should be placed within the organization. Organizational analysis consists of the following elements:
   - **Analysis of Objectives:** The long-term and short-term objectives and their relative priorities are analyzed. Specific goals and strategies for various departments and sections should be stated as means for achieving the overall organizational objectives. General objectives need to be translated into specific and detailed operational targets. It is also necessary to continuously review and revise the objectives in the light of the changing environment.
   - **Resource Utilization Analysis:** The allocation of human and physical resources and their efficient utilization in meeting the operational targets are analyzed. In order to examine in detail the inputs and outputs of the organization, efficiency indices may be developed. These indices will help to determine the adequacy of specific work flow as well as the contribution of human resources.
   - **Organizational Climate Analysis:** The prevailing climate of an organization reflects the member's attitudes. It also represents management attitude towards employee development. Without adequate management support and appropriate supervisory styles, a training programme cannot be successful. Analysis of Organization climate can reveal the strengths and weaknesses also.
   - **Environmental Scanning:** The economic, political, technological and socio-cultural environments are examined. Both the internal and external factors affect the working of an organization. The internal factors are controllable and the external factors are uncontrollable in nature.

2. **Task or Role Analysis:** It is a systematic and detailed analysis of jobs to identify job contents, the knowledge, skills and aptitudes required and the work behavior. On the part of the job holder, particular attention should be paid to the task to be performed, the methods to be used, the way employees have learned these methods and the performance standards required of employees. It is also called operational analysis; its purpose is to decide what should be taught. Questionnaire, interviews, human resource records, reports, tests, observation and other methods can be used to collect information about jobs in the organization.

3. **Manpower Analysis:** In this analysis, the persons to be trained and the changes required in the knowledge, skills and aptitudes of an employee are determined. First of all, it is necessary to decide whether performance of an individual is sub-standard and training is needed? Secondly it is determined whether the employee is capable of being trained. Lastly whether the training will improve employees' performance or not is determined. Other alternatives to training e.g. modifications, observation, supervisory evaluation, work samples, diagnostic tests and performance reports provide the information needed to choose from these alternatives. Training can be relevant and viable if three types of analysis above are carried on continuously. Moreover, these analyses should be integrated in a carefully designed and executed programme.

Training needs may be discovered /identified for the new as well as the present employees and for solving the specific problem in the following ways:

(1) **Identifying specific problems:** Such problems are productivity; high costs, poor material and control, poor quality, excessive scrap and waste, excessive management-labour troubles, grievances, violation of rules of conduct, poor discipline, high employee turnover and transfers, absenteeism, accidents, excessive fatigue and fumbling, discouragement, struggling with the job, standards of performance not met and delayed production. Problems like these suggest that training may be necessary.

(2) **Anticipating impending and future problems:** Bearing on the expansion of business, the introduction of new products, new services, new designs, new plant, new technology and of organizational changes concerned with manpower inventory for present and future needs.

(3) **Managers and supervisors may make specific request for setting training programmes:** Though this method is simple and a correct evaluation of employees performance deficiencies can be made, but often such recommendations may be built on faulty assumptions and requests may not coincide with each other or organizational goals.

(4) **Interviewing and observing the personnel on the job:** Interviewing personnel and direct questioning and observation of employee by his superiors may also reveal training needs.

(5) An analysis of the past performance records of the perspective trainee and comparing his actual performance with the target performance may provide clues to specific interpersonal skills that may need development.

(6) Questionnaires may be used for eliciting opinions of the employees on topics like communication ,satisfaction, job characteristics, their attitude towards working conditions, pay, promotion policies, etc. these will reveal much information about where an employee's skills and knowledge are deficient.

Training Needs Can Further be Identified as per the Following:

Analyzing the training needs provides a focus and direction for the investment that an organization must make to develop its people. Training needs assessment help to (a) pin point whether training will make a difference in productivity and the bottom line, (b) decide what specific training each employee needs and what will be improve the job performance, and (c) differentiate between the need for training and organizational issues.

There are many techniques, different from one another, for collecting data relating to job performance. There are four major approaches to accommodate the techniques – meeting managers, interviews, desk researches, and self – complete questionnaire.

Several basic training needs assessments techniques include:

- **Meeting Managers:** You can meet the managers to enquire about the achievement of business goals and the involvement of the supervisors with the planning of projects and the future of the company. They know what will be needed. Managers will communicate where their employee's current abilities lie and what is needed to get them to the next level for new projects on the horizon.
- **Questionnaires:** You are required to design a questionnaire and administer it to the employees, and to the immediate supervisor, to be aware of the shortcomings of an employee. Consultation with person in key position, and/or with specific knowledge, will help you in decision making.
- **Review of Company Goals:** A brief review of the company's past and where they are headed for the future may reveal valuable information for training. A comparison should be made of what employees are currently doing and what will be expected of them as the company continues to grow and change.
- **Focus Groups:** You can ask the employees to discuss what difficulties they may be facing from day to day and what would make their job easier and more efficient. Remember to keep them focused on what they need rather than on what they want. You should discuss with the line managers about recorded points.
- **Records and Report Studies:** You can get valuable information from various records, for example, performance appraisal reports, performance review reports, HR audit reports, gap analysis records, and the like.
- **HR Audit Reports:** The report (a) examines and pin points strengths and weakness related to HR area and skills, and competencies to enable an organization to achieve its

long-terms and short-terms goals, (b) increases the effectiveness of the design and implementation of human resource policies planning, and programmes, and (c) helps human resource planners develop and update employment programme plans. Thus, you can assess the training needs referring to the audit reports.

Tools of Identifying Training Needs

Job requirement, employees' job skills, analysis of the activities, and the situation in which the activities are formed, and other aspects are the tools of determining training needs. Some of these are:

- **Analysis of Activity:** The analysis of activity lists the activities required in manufacturing a product or offering service or part thereof, in a logical sequence and then determine what new competency, knowledge, or skill is required to successfully accomplish the product or service. This analysis also helps to find out necessary modification of present knowledge or skill.
- **Analysis of the Problem:** If any task is performed without any problem or the problem remain hidden, then this analysis is not called for. But, in case of emergence of a problem, this analysis is done to identify the root cause behind the problem and to ascertain the knowledge or skill or both in addition to the insights required.
- **Analysis of behavior:** Some potential employees sometimes behave differently. Analysis of the typical behavior by individuals or groups provides the opportunity to determine the corrective action involving training.
- **Analysis of Organisation:** Organisational diagnosis and analysis of organizational weakness provides clues to identify individual and group training needs.
- **Appraisal of performance:** Analysis of performance through formal performance appraisal or in formal performance review helps determine whether someone lacks something, be it additional knowledge, skill, or understanding colleagues or the situation.
- **Brainstorming:** This is a unique technique of total quality management. It is used in many other disciplines. A group of homogeneous people from the workplace meets to generate new ideas around a specific area of interest. Using brainstorming rules, which remove inhibitions, people are able to think more freely and move into new areas of thought and so create numerous new ideas and solutions. The participants shout out ideas as they occur to them and also build on the ideas raised by others. One contributes the idea only when his/her turn comes in a case systematic brainstorming session. All the ideas are noted down and are not criticized during the 'idea collection' stage. Only when the brainstorming session is over, are the ideas evaluated. Brainstorming helps to identify training needs from the answers to the questions.
- **Buzzing:** Refers to interacting with the seniors, peers, and junior colleagues on 'what additional areas of knowledge do we need to handle the work better?'

- **Card Sort:** Statement or potential training needs are first return on cards given to the participating members, whose ideas are sought. They arrange the cards in the order of importance.
- **Checklist:** A whole job, process, programme, or area of responsibility is broken down into detailed parts or activities and arranged in logical sequence. Each person likely to be engaged in the job, checks the list to identify the additional inputs (knowledge or skill) that he/she needs to successfully accomplish the work.
- **Comparison:** This involves comparing what an individual is doing and what else he/she is being asked to do.
- **Conference:** Discussion on decision making on training needs identification.
- **Consultants:** If the task is critical and not so familiar, then an external consultant is engaged to identify the training needs.
- **Counselling:** It refers to discussion between a training practitioner and the person seeking guidance. A Counsellor listens attentively to what the person says and works to define the goals with respect to the values and culture, appreciate the thoughts, feelings and worries about a situation, and helps to gain insight into how to act, think and feel. The counsellor teaches, shows, and helps the person to express emotions in his/her own way and workout solutions to problems, and guides and supports the person in his/her needs. Most importantly, the counsellor uses a variety of techniques to help the person explore what is important and to become empowered to act in ways that are in his/her best interest.
- **In-Basket:** Managers are facing problems everyday. In-basket is used to test the manager's ability to handle the problems. The problems come to the in-box from various sources. The in-box may be electronic, say, through intranet, LAN, WAN, or e-mail.

Case Study

UNDERSTANDING PARTICIPANT NEEDS

Magna Synthetics: Magna Synthetics is a growing company employing about 1250 employees. The company came into existence in 1988. Its product range includes linen, yarn and twines, lyocell fibers, pure wool and blended yarns, wood combing, linen and flax canvases, and certain by-products. Over the years it has increased its product range, penetrated new markets, and captured new customer. The company, keeping track with the changes in the business scenario, has upgraded its technology and purchased new generation machines. While implementing new technology, Magnus Synthetics encountered resistance to change from unions and majority of employees. As such the company felt the utmost necessity of educating the workforce. Furthermore, the need for organizing training programmes in the field of technology emerged as vital.

The company established its training division in 1995, headed by a full time training manager. Mr. Prasad had worked in planning, production, maintenance, and quality control. Considering his experience in cross-functional areas Mr. Prasad was relieved from other responsibilities and assigned the task of developing the training department. Moreover, he was a training-minded officer and in meetings, he advocated the need of training for organizational growth.

The training division started functioning. It initially planned to organize a few induction programmes for new recruits who had joined in the proceeding six months. It successfully conducted three such programmes to induct forty-three employees. Company history, principle products, customers, financial position, achievements and growth, future plans, technology in use, plans to upgrade technology, and prospective customers, etc. were included in the curriculum. All the trained employees were delighted.

The division launched an in-house course of working persons. It stratified the employees based on the levels, functional areas, and length of service rendered. Initially, it planned to conduct a course for persons with ten years experience in a particular production department. The duration of the training was 60 hours spread over twenty working days, for 3 hours per day in the afternoon. The employees thought that they would get doubts clarified and get responses to unanswered questions; each employee had some difficulties in his/her work area.

The training department received nominations from departments. The age of the nominees ranged from 29-45 years, the average age being 39 years. Considering the length of experience, experts in the field were invited to share their knowledge and experiences. Managers of Magna Synthetics were also detailed for some classes. The employees were delighted. For most of them this was their first training session after joining the company. But, gradually, they lost interest as was seen from their late arrivals, desire to leave early, yawning, pale faces, and the like.

Once, during tea break, a faculty member was initially pre-occupied with exchanging training-related information but the direction of discussion changed into exchanging personal information. The discussion, aimed at rapport building was progressing smoothly. During the conversation, the faculty casually asked about his style of teaching and requested an honest opinion. The participants, very diplomatically, first highlighted the strong points and then mentioned about one weak point, namely, traces of stammering. The faculty member did not take this sportingly. He offered little advice to the participant and preceded the faculty room.

During the valediction of the training programme, the training manager observed the facial expressions and made his readings. The training division collected feedback from the employees. The training feedback format contained a name field. The grades in the format ranged from excellent, very good, good, fair, and poor. Internal faculty members received the grading, very good or good. But the seven external faculty members, only one received excellent, two were very good, three were fair and one was just as poor.

Q. Is providing training as per the employee's needs important and useful?

Summary

This chapter is concerned with the psychology of learning and learned motivation. It gives a view of the laws, principles and theories of learning along with learned motivation. It also explains the learning patterns, characteristics of learning and climate for learning. It also explains in detail the identification of training needs in an organization through organizational analysis, task or role analysis, and manpower analysis. And also the tools for identifying training needs are described.

Concept Review Questions

OBJECTIVES

1. __________ is the process of encoding, retaining, and using information.
2. __________ of message builds a pattern into one's memory.
3. Learning is __________ and not passive.
4. Previous __________ of the individual trainee affects his learning experiences.
5. Learning is closely related to __________ and __________.
6. __________are important ingredient in the learning environment.
7. Better informed workers are less likely to make __________mistakes.
8. __________ can help prevent industrial accidents.

(Learning, Repetition, active, experience, attention/ concentration, Trainers, operational, Training)

SHORT QUESTIONS

1. What do mean by learning?
2. What are the various laws of learning?
3. What are the various principles of learning?
4. How will you identify the training need in an organization?
5. What do you mean by organizational analysis and what are its important components?
6. Write short notes on:
   (*a*) resource utilization analysis
   (*b*) organizational climate analysis
   (*c*) environmental scanning
7. "Learning is good for everyone". Discuss.
8. Differentiate between manpower and task analysis?

LONG QUESTIONS

1. What do you mean by learning and what are its important laws?
2. How can we assess the need for training in an organization?
3. Explain in detail the various theories of learning?
4. What are the various tools which can be used for identifying training needs?
5. What do you mean by manpower analysis?
6. What do mean by role or task analysis?
7. Write a detailed note on organizational analysis.
8. What are the various types of analysis required in the identification of training needs?

3

Career Planning

TRAINING OBJECTIVES

Training objectives are some kind of statements of what training is expected to achieve. Setting training objectives must be accurate because of the training is one of the important function in human resources management and also it is a costly process.

So the training objectives should be expected level of an employee by employer.

The setting objectives of training, depends on the organization. It may differ from an organization to organization. In an organization the objectives basically depends on its vision, mission and corporate objectives.

These have to be achieved without any argument. But in operational level, there can be identified most of times when employees make lots of mistakes because of the lack of training. Even they are highly paid, highly motivated people; this can not be decreased to large amounts. Following type of situations are the indicators of the training needs and the training objectives.

- Training objectives should achieve and fulfill training needs of an organization.
- Also training objectives should have a power of motivation. Otherwise if the training objectives make stress on the employee, then the out come of training may not achieve the objectives.
- The training objective clears what goals have to be achieved by the end of training program i.e. what the trainees are expected to be able to do at the end of their training.
- Training objectives assist trainers to design the training program.

Designing Training Objectives

Generally line managers ask the personnel manager to formulate the training policies. The personnel manager formulates the following training objectives keeping in view the company's goals and objectives;

(*a*) To prepare the employee both new and old to meet the present as well as the changing requirements of the job and the organisation.

(*b*) To prevent obsolescence.

(*c*) To impart the new entrants the basic knowledge and skill they need for an intelligent performance of definite job.

(*d*) To prepare employees for higher level tasks.

(*e*) To assist employees to function more effectively in their present positions by exposing them to the latest concepts, information and techniques and developing the skills they will need in their particular field.

(*f*) To build up a second line of competent officers and prepare them to occupy more responsible positions.

(*g*) To broaden the minds of senior managers by providing them with opportunities for an interchange of experiences within and outside with a view to correcting the narrowness of outlook that may arise from over-specialization.

(*h*) To develop the potentialities of people for the next level job.

(*i*) To ensure smooth and efficient working of a department.

(*j*) To ensure economical output of required quality.

(k) To promote individual and collective morale, a sense of responsibility, co-operative attitude and good relationships.

Training Methods and Techniques

The methods of training are basically divided into two parts i.e. on –the job training method and off-the job training method. These methods are as given below:

On-The Job Training Methods	***Off-The Job Training Methods***
Job-Instruction Training	Simulation
Apprentice Training	• Vestibule Training
Job Rotation	• Role Playing
Coaching	• Case Study
Committee Assignments	• Sensitivity Training
	Conference
	Seminar or Discussion
	Audio Visuals
	Programmed Instruction
	Lecture

A. ON-THE JOB TRAINING METHODS

On the job training is the most commonly used method of training. Under this method, the individual is placed on a regular job and taught the skills necessary to perform that job. Majority of industrial training is of on-the-job training type.

It is informal, as the trainee learns under the supervision and guidance of a qualified worker or instructor. Trainees earn as they learn under the watchful eyes of a master mechanic or craftsman, receive immediate feedback, practice in the actual work environment, and associate with the same people they will work with after training.

Under this technique the employee is placed in a new job and is told how it may be performed. It is primarily concerned with developing in an employee a repertoire of skills and habits consistent with the existing practices of an organization, and with orienting him to his immediate problems.

Advantages

The Major Advantages of On-the Job Training Are as Follows:

- The main advantage of on-the job training is that the trainee learns on the actual equipment in use and the true environment of his job.
- While the trainee learns how to perform a job, he is also a regular worker rendering the services for which he is paid.
- The problem of transfer of a trainee is also minimized as the person is on-the job.
- It is highly economical since no additional personnel or facilities are required for training.
- The trainee learns the rules, regulations, procedures, by observing their day to day applications.
- This type of training is suitable alternative for a company in which there are almost most as many jobs as there are employees.
- Finally, it is more appropriate for teaching the knowledge and skills which can be acquired in a relatively short period say, a few days or weeks.

Disadvantages

The Major Disadvantages of On-the Job of Training Are as Follows:

- On-the job training suffers from certain disadvantages as well. The principal disadvantage of on-the job training is that the instruction is often disorganized and haphazard and not properly supervised. This is due to such reasons as the inability of the experienced employee to impart skills to the trainee, the breakdown of the job for the purpose of instructions, and the lack of motivation of the part of the trainee to receive training.
- Moreover, learners are often subjected to distractions of a noisy shop or office.
- In addition, a poorly conducted on-the job training programme is likely to create safety hazards, result in damaged products or materials, and bring unnecessary stress to the trainees.
- Further the other drawback is the low productivity, especially when the employee is unable to fully develop his skills.

The Methods Of On-The Job Training Are As Follows:

1. JOB-INSTRUCTION TRAINING (JIT)

This is the first method of on-the job training. This method is very popular in the states for preparing supervisors to train operatives. The JIT method requires skilled trainers, extensive job analysis, training schedules, and prior assessment of the trainee's job knowledge. This method is also known as "training through step by step learning."

It involves listing all necessary steps in the job, each in proper sequence. The actual training follows a four-step process, beginning with:

(1) The preparation of the trainee for instruction. This includes putting him at ease, emphasizing the importance of the task and giving a general description of job, duties and responsibilities.

(2) Presentation of the instructions, giving essential information in a clear manner. This includes positioning the trainee at work site , telling and showing him each step of the job, stressing why and how each step is carried out as it is shown;

(3) Having the trainee try out the job to show that he has understood the instructions, If there are any errors they are corrected; and

(4) Encouraging questions and allowing the trainee to work along and the trainer follows up regularly.

Advantages

The Advantages Of Job-Instruction Training Are As Follows:

- The JIT method provides immediate feedback on results, quick correction of errors and provision for extra practice when required.

- This is a popular method to train supervisors to train operatives.
- It gives detailed and clear cut information to the trainee and helps in increasing knowledge.
- It also helps in encouraging questions and allowing the trainee to work with co-ordination.

Disadvantages

The disadvantages of job-instruction training are as follows:

- It demands skilled trainer and can interfere with production and quality.
- This is a lengthy process as this method is "training through step by step learning."
- This method is costly as it requires skilled trainers, extensive job analysis, training schedules, and prior assessment of the trainee's job knowledge.

2. APPRENTICESHIP

The second important method of on-the job training is apprenticeship. The Apprentice Act, 1961 requires industrial units of specified industries to provide training on basic skills and knowledge in specified trades to educated employees/apprentices with a view to improving their employment opportunities or to enable them to start their own industry.

For training in crafts, trades and in technical areas, apprenticeship training is the oldest and most commonly used method, especially when proficiency in a job is the result of relatively long period of 2 to 3 years for persons of superior ability and from 4 years to 5 years for others.

The field in which apprenticeship training is offered are numerous and range from the job of a printer, a tool-maker, a pattern designer, a mechanic, carpenters, weavers, fitters, jewellers, engravers, and electricians etc.

A major part of training time is spent on-the job productive work. Each apprentice is given a programme of assignments according to a predetermined schedule, which provides for efficient training in trade skills.

Advantages

The advantages of apprenticeship training are as follows:

- A skilled workforce is maintained and is facilitated in number of skills.
- Immediate returns can be expected from training because the trainees will be immediately observed to the job.
- The workmanship and response will be very good.
- The hiring cost is lower because of reduced turnover and lower production costs.
- The loyalty of employees is increased and opportunities for growth are frequent.

Disadvantages

The disadvantages of apprenticeship training are as follows:

- It is technical based training and limited to certain fields only.
- It is a time consuming and lengthy method of training.
- It is a expensive method and ensures no guarantee about the success.

3. JOB ROTATION

This is the third most important method of on-the job training. Job rotation refers to moving employees from job to job to add variety and reduce boredom by allowing them to perform a variety of tasks. When an activity is no longer challenging, the employees would be moved to another job at the same level that has similar skill requirements.

The trainee receives the job knowledge and gains experience from his supervisor or trainer in each of the different job assignments.

Though this method of training is common in training managers for general management positions, trainees can also be rotated from job to job in workshop jobs.

This method gives an opportunity to the trainee to understand the problems of employees on other jobs and respect them.

Advantages

The advantages of job-rotation training are as follows:

- It reduces boredom and disinterest through diversifying the employee's activities.
- Employees with a wider range of skills give the management more flexibility in scheduling work.
- It also helps in adapting to changes and filing vacancies.
- Competition can be stimulated by rotation.
- It also stimulates more co-operative attitude.
- It provides general background of business as a whole.

Disadvantages

The disadvantages of job-rotation training are as follows:

- Job rotation also has its drawbacks as the training costs are increased.
- It leads to disruption of work as the rotated employees take time to adjust to a new set up.
- It can also de-motivate intelligent and ambitious trainees who seek specific responsibilities in their chosen speciality.
- Productive works of almost all the departments suffer due to interruptions in all departments.

4. COACHING

The fourth method of on-the job training is coaching. Employees are coached and instructed by skilled co-workers, by supervisors, by the special training instructors.

They learn the job by personnel observation and practice as well as occasionally handling it.

It is learning by doing, and it is most useful for jobs that are difficult to stimulate or can be learned quickly by watching and doing.

Advantages

The advantages of coaching method are as follows:

- The trainee shares some of the duties and the responsibilities of the coach and relieves him of his burden.
- The supervisor provides feedback to the trainee on his performance and offers him some suggestions for improvement.
- This method is useful for the employees as they are coached and instructed by trained instructors.

Disadvantages

The disadvantages of coaching method are as follows:

- A limitation of this method of training is that the trainee may not have the freedom or opportunity to express his own ideas.
- This method is also disadvantageous because employee learns the job by personnel observation and practice so it consumes a lot of time.
- It is a costly method of training as it requires special training instructors who are well trained in their fields.

5. COMMITTEE ASSIGNMENTS

This is another important method of on-the job training. Under the committee assignments, group of trainees are given and asked to solve an actual organizational problem.

Special assignments or committees are methods used to provide lower level executives with first hand experience in working on actual problems.

Executives from various functional areas serve on 'boards' and are required to analyze problems and recommend solutions to the top management.

Advantages

The advantages of committee assignments are as follows:

- Committee assignments are advantageous as they develop team work.
- It is also beneficial for the employees as they gain experience by solving actual problems.
- It is a useful method which provides first hand experience to the lower level executives.
- It also develops co-ordination and co-operation among the employees.

Disadvantages

The disadvantages of committee assignments are as follows:

- As the employees solve the problems jointly at times it leads to difference of opinions.
- There is lack of co-ordination due to mutual conflicts.
- The new employees are unable to analyze the problems accurately.
- The decisions taken may not be appropriate.

B. OFF-THE JOB TRAINING METHODS

Under this method of training, trainee is separated from the job situation and his attention is focused upon learning the material related to his future job performance.

Since the trainee is not distracted by job requirements, he can place his entire concentration on learning the job rather than spending his time in performing it.

Advantages

The major advantages of off-the job training are as follows:

- There is an opportunity for freedom of expression for the trainees.
- In this method the focus is upon learning the material and related future job performance.
- The trainee is not distracted by job requirements and he can focus properly and can place his entire concentration on learning.

Disadvantages

The major disadvantages of off-the job training are as follows:

- As the trainee is separated from the job situation so there is loss of work.
- It is a time consuming process.
- Development is regarded of primary importance and the work is of secondary importance as per this method of training.

The Methods of Off-the Job Training Are as Follows:

1. SIMULATION

It is one of the important methods of off-the job training. Simulation is a technique that duplicates as nearly as possible the actual conditions encountered on the job. Simulation then, is an attempt to create a realistic decision making environment for the trainee.

Simulations present likely problem situations and decision alternatives to the trainee. For example, activities of an organization may be simulated and the trainee may be asked to make a decision in support of those activities. The results of those decisions are reported back to the trainee with an explanation of what would have happened, had they actually been made in the work place.

Advantages

The advantages of simulation method of training are as follows:

- The trainee learns from this feedback and improves his/her subsequent simulation and work place decisions.
- Instant feedback is provided to the trainees for their betterment.
- Simulation helps in creating a realistic decision making environment for the trainee.

Disadvantages

The disadvantages of simulation method of training are as follows:

- Simulation is a technique that duplicates as nearly as possible the actual conditions encountered on the job but it is not actual.
- The decisions may not accurate as the trainees are not experienced enough.
- It is a complex method.

• VESTIBULE TRAINING

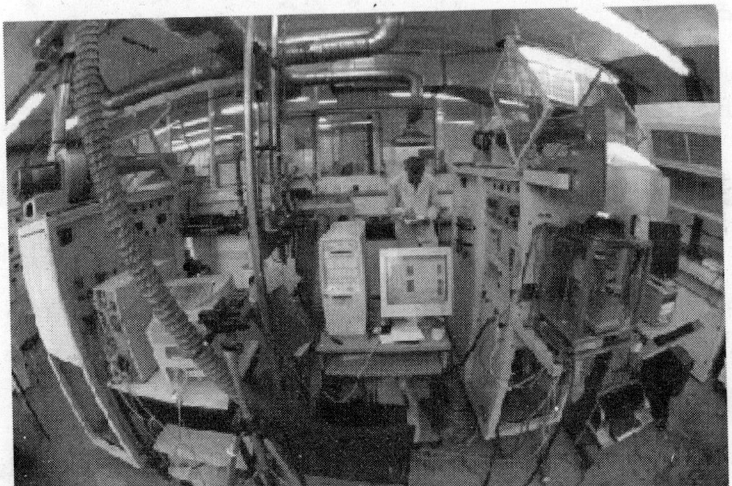

Another important method of off-the job training is vestibule training. This method attempts to duplicate on –the job situations in a company classroom. Vestibule training utilizes equipment which closely resembles the actual ones used on the job. This technique enables the trainee to concentrate on learning the skill rather than on performing an actual job. Theoretical training is given in the classroom, while the practical work is conducted in the production line.

A special area or a room is set aside from the main production area and is equipped with furnishings similar to those found in the actual production area.

The trainee is then permitted to learn under simulated conditions, without disrupting ongoing operations. The emphasis is on learning the skills required by the job.

It is a very efficient method of training semi-skilled personnel, particularly when employees have to be trained for the same kind of work at the same time.

It is often used to train clerks, bank tellers, inspectors, operators, testers, typists, etc. The duration ranges from days to weeks. Theory can be related to practice in this method.

Advantages

The advantages of vestibule training method are as follows:

- A primary advantage of vestibule training is that it relieves the employee from the pressure of having to produce while learning.
- Training is given in a separate room, distractions are minimized.
- A trained instructor, who knows how to teach, can be more effectively utilized.
- The correct method can be taught without interrupting production.
- It permits the trainee to practice without the fear of supervisor's observation and their possible ridicule.

Disadvantages

The disadvantages of vestibule training method are as follows:

- It is difficult to duplicate the pressures and realities of actual decision making on the job.
- Individuals often act differently in real life situations than they do in acting out a simulated exercise.
- The splitting of responsibilities leads to organizational problems.

§ This method is of the limited value for the job which can be duplicated.

§ High costs are incurred in creating artificial environment.

• Role Playing

This method was developed by **Moreno, a Venetian psychiatrist**. He coined the terms "role playing," "role reversal," "socio-drama," "psycho-drama," and a variety of specialized terms, with emphasis on learning human relation skills through practice and insight into one's own behavior and its affect on others.

It has been defined as "a method of human interaction which involves realistic behavior in the imaginary situations." As (**Norman**) has pointed out, a "role playing experience soon demonstrates the gap between 'thinking' and 'doing'. The idea of role playing involves action, doing, and practice.

It is also defined as a method of human interactions that involve realistic behavior in imaginary situations. The participants play the role of certain characters such as the production manager, mechanical engineer, superintendent, maintenance engineers, quality and control inspectors, foreman, workers and the like.

In role playing, trainees act out a given role as they would in a stage play. Two or more trainees are assigned parts to play before the rest of the class. These parts do not involve any memorization of lines or any rehearsals.

The role players are simply informed of a situation and of the respective roles they have to play. Sometime after the preliminary planning, the situation is acted out by the role players.

Role playing primarily involves employee-employer relationships hiring, firing, discussing a grievance procedure, conducting a post-appraisal interview or disciplining a subordinate or a salesman making a presentation to a Customer.

Advantages

The advantages of role playing method of training are as follows:

- Role playing helps promote inter-personnel relations.
- Attitude change is another result of role playing and it also leads to understanding among individuals.
- It develops skills and ability to apply knowledge, particularly in areas like human relations.
- It also develops the tendency in employees of how to control the situations.

Disadvantages:

The disadvantages of role playing method of training are as follows:

- Role playing is not an easy task as it requires efficient executives.
- It is organized just to increase the trainee's skill in dealing with other people i.e. particularly development of human relations and decision making ability.
- It is a narrow and a complex method.
- It is not as effective as multiple role-playing.

• Case Study

Case study is also a method of off-the job training. This method was first developed in the 1800s by **Christopher Lang dell** at the Harvard Law School to help students. A case study is a written description of an actual situation in business which provokes, in the reader, the need to decide what is going on, what the situation really is or what the problems are, and what can and should be done.

The 'case' is a set of data (real or frictional), written or oral miniature description and summary of such data that presents, issues and problem calling for solutions or action on the part of the trainee. When the trainees are given cases to analyze, they are asked to identify the problem and recommend tentative solutions for it.

This method offers to the trainees matter for reflection and brings home to them a sense of the complexity of life as opposed to theoretical simplifications of, and practices in the decision making process. It Diagnoses and deals with real life situations.

The case study is primarily useful as a training technique for supervisors and is specially valuable as a technique of developing decision making skills and for broadening the perspective of the trainee.

The person in charge of training, makes out a case, provides the necessary explanations, initiates the discussion going ; and then, once the discussion gets going, he intervenes as little as possible.

In the incident method, a full detailed description of a situation is not given. The trainer merely presents an outline, often in the form of a complaint from a costumer or a severe conflict in the management of a business. The trainee arrives at the facts in issue by asking questions from the trainer or finding out a solution by 'acting out' the situation in which a trainee plays a role.

Example of Case Study

- Is Rajat in need of Remedial Training?

Rajat Sharma has been employed for six months in the accounts section of a large manufacturing company in Faridabad. You have been his supervisor for the past three months. Recently you have been asked by the management to find out the contributions of each employee in the Accounts Section and monitor carefully whether they are meeting the standards set by you.

A few days back you have completed your formal investigation and with the exception of Rajat, all seem to be meeting the targets set by you. Along with numerous errors, Rajat's work is characterized by low performance – often he does 20 percent less than the other clerks in the department.

As you look into Rajat's performance review sheets again, you begin to wonder whether some sort of remedial training is needed for people like him.

Questions

1. As Rajat's supervisor can you find out whether the poor performance is due to poor training or to some other cause?
2. If you find Rajat has been inadequately trained, how do you go about introducing a remedial training programme?
3. If he has been with the company for six months, what kind of remedial programme would be best?
4. Should you supervise him more closely? Can you do this without making it obvious to him and his co-workers?
5. Should you discuss the situation with Rajat?

Advantages

The advantages of case study method are as follows:

- It promotes analytical thinking and develops a person's problem solving ability.
- Since cases are usually based on real problem situations the trainees' interest in them tends to be very great.
- It encourages open mindedness and serves as a means of integrating the knowledge obtained from different basic disciplines.
- It is a valuable technique as it helps in developing decision making skills and broadening the perspective of the trainee.

Disadvantages

The disadvantages of case study method are as follows:

- It may degenerate into a mere dreary demonstration of dusty museum pieces, if it is taught only from books at developing centers of learning.
- The preparation of cases is difficult, for it needs money and time, and it is not quite certain that the outcome of this method would be worth the expenditure in money and men incurred on it.
- This method is based on predictions therefore not much reliable.

• SENSITIVITY TRAINING

One of the most important methods of off-the job training is sensitivity training. (**Bethel Maine of USA**) was pioneer of this method. It is an experimental approach to training. Sensitivity training uses small numbers of trainees, usually fewer than 12 in a group. They meet with a passive trainer and gain insight into their own and others behavior. Meetings have no agenda, are held away from work places and questions deal with the 'here and now' of the group process.

Sensitivity training is a group training method that uses intensive participation and gives immediate feedback for self analysis and change.

The effectiveness of this method depends upon the ability of the participant to apply concepts and awareness obtained in the laboratory or group to his job, the transfer of his knowledge to the organization is possible if the organization has an open culture, an atmosphere of open discussion, encourage conflict resolution and promote mutual trust.

Sensitivity training can go by a variety of names-laboratory training, encounter groups or T-groups. It was considered necessary that to change behavior, imparting necessary skills is required.

Advantages

The advantages of sensitivity training are as follows:

- Sensitivity training is a group training method that uses intensive participation and gives immediate feedback for self analysis and change.
- T-group training is process oriented and not content oriented where people operate from a level of communication, observing, revealing, listening, and unraveling messages.
- Managerial sensitivity is increased.
- It involves face to face learning about original behaviour in a small group.
- It leads to promotion of mutual trust.

Disadvantages

The disadvantages of sensitivity training are as follows:

- The effectiveness of this method depends upon the ability of the participant to apply concepts and awareness obtained in the laboratory or group to his job.
- It is a artificial method.
- The transfer of knowledge to the organization is possible if the organization has an open culture.
- As the meetings have no agenda, and are held away from work places so a lot of expenditure is incurred.

2. CONFERENCE

This is another method of off-the job training. In this method, the participating individuals 'confer' to discuss points of common interest to each other. A conference is basic to most participative group centered methods of development.

It is a formal meeting conducted in accordance with an organized plan, in which the leader seeks to develop knowledge and understanding by obtaining a considerable amount of oral participation of the trainees.

It lays emphasis on small group discussions, on organized subject matter, and on the active participation of the members involved. Learning is facilitated by building up on the ideas contributed by the conferees.

There are three types of conferences. In the directed discussion, the trainer guides the discussion in such a way that the facts, principles or concepts are explained.

In the training conference, the instructor gets the group to pool its knowledge and past experience and brings different points of view to clear the problem.

In the seminar conference, answer is bound to a question or a solution to a problem. For this, the instructor defines the problem, encourages and ensures full participation in the discussion.

Advantages

The advantages of conference training are as follows:

- The conference is ideally suited for the purpose of analyzing problems and issues and examining them from different view points.
- It is an excellent method for the development of conceptual knowledge and for reducing dogmatism and modifying attitudes because the participants develops solutions and reach conclusions which they often willingly accept.
- One can learn from others by comparing his own opinion with that of others.
- The trainee is also taught to respect others.
- It is the most participative group centered methods of development.

Disadvantages

The disadvantages of conference training are as follows:

- It is limited to a small group of 15 -20 persons, because larger groups often discourage the active participation of all the conferees.
- The process is usually slow because all those desiring to speak on a point are generally allowed to do so. Consequently irrelevant issues easily creep in.
- There are also differences of opinions among the members of the group.

3. SEMINAR OR DISCUSSION

Off-the job training can also be provided through seminar or discussion. It is a method used for training the clerical, professional and supervisory personnel. This method involves a group of people who pose ideas, examine and share facts, ideas and data, test assumptions and draw conclusions, which contribute to the improvement of job performance.

It may be based on paper prepared by one or more trainees on a subject selected in consultation with the person in charge of the seminar. It may be a part of a study or related to theoretical studies or practical problems. The trainees read their papers, and this is followed by a critical discussion.

The chairman of the seminar summarizes the contents of the papers and the discussions which follow their reading. The person in charge of the seminar distributes in advance the materials to be analyzed in the form of required readings.

Valuable working material may be provided to the trainees by actual files. The trainees may consult the files and bring these to the seminar where they may study in detail the various aspects and complexities of a particular job or work or task.

Advantages

The advantages of seminar or discussions are as follows:

§ The seminar compares the reactions of trainees, encourages discussion, defines the general trends and guides the participants to certain conclusions.

- Discussion involves two way communications and hence feedback is provided.
- The participants feel free to speak in small groups.
- Valuable working material is provided to the trainees.
- It is also helpful in improving the job performance.

Disadvantages

The disadvantages of seminar or discussions are as follows:

- The success of this method depends on the leadership qualities of the person who leads the group.
- There might be conflicts in individual's opinions.
- Some trainees may not take the initiative to speak out their views.

4. AUDIO VISUALS

Another method of off-the job training are audio visuals. Audio visuals include television, slides, overheads, videotapes and films. These can be used to provide a wide range of realistic examples of job conditions and situations in the condensed period of time.

Further, the quality of the presentation can be controlled and will remain equal for all training groups.

Advantages

The advantages of audio visuals are as follows:

- It is an interesting and effective method.
- The quality of presentation can be controlled and will remain equal for all training groups.
- Wide range of examples of job conditions can be provided in a shorter period of time.
- As there is the use of television, slides, overheads, video tapes and films the trainees show keen interest.

Disadvantages

The disadvantages of audio visuals are as follows:

- Audio visuals constitute a one-way system of communication with no scope for the audience to raise doubts for clarification.
- There is no flexibility of presentation from audience to audience.
- All the important information cannot be displayed through audio visual aids.

5. PROGRAMMED INSTRUCTIONS

Off-the job training also uses programmed instruction as an appropriate method. This is a method where training is offered without the intervention of a trainer. Information is provided to the trainee in blocks, either in a book form or through a teaching machine.

After reading each block of material the learner must answer a question about it. Feedback in the form of correct answers is provided after each response.

The programme involves: presenting question, facts or problems to the trainee to utilize the information given; and the trainee instantly receive feedback on the basis of the accuracy of his answers.

Advantages

The advantages of programmed instructions are as follows:

- As it is self paced the trainees can progress through the programmes at their own speed.
- Strong motivation is provided to the learner to repeat learning.
- The materials to be learned are broken down into small units. The material is also self structured and self contained, offering scope for practice.

Disadvantages

The disadvantages of programmed instructions are as follows:

- The scope for learning is less, compared to other methods of training.
- Cost of preparing books, manuals and machinery is considerably high.
- Philosophical and attitudinal concepts and motor skills cannot be taught by this method.

6. LECTURE

Another method of off-the job training is the lecture method. Lecture is a verbal presentation of information by an instructor to a large audience.

Lectures are regarded as one of the simplest ways of imparting knowledge to the trainees, specially when facts, concepts or principles, attitudes, theories and problem solving abilities are to be taught. The lecture is presumed to possess a considerable depth of knowledge of subject at hand.

Advantages

The advantages of lecture method are as follows:

- The virtue of this method is that it can be used for very large groups, and hence the cost per trainee is low.
- This method is helpful in imparting technical or special information of a complex nature.

Disadvantages

The disadvantages of lecture method are as follows:

- This method violates the principle of learning by practice hence it leads to the lack of practice.
- It constitutes a one-way communication.
- There is no feedback from the audience.
- Continuous lecturing is likely to bore the audience.
- It is a lengthy method of training

TRAINING DESIGN

The design of the training program can be undertaken only when a clear training objective has been produced. The training objective clears what goal has to be achieved by the end of training program i.e. what the trainees are expected to be able to do at the end of their training. Training objectives assist trainers to design the training program.

- **The Trainer:** Before starting a training program, a trainer analyzes his technical, interpersonnel, judgmental skills in order to deliver quality content to trainers.
- **The Trainees:** A good training design requires close scrutiny of the trainees and their profiles. Age, experience, needs and expectations of the trainees are some of the important factors that affect training design.
- **Training Climate:** A good training climate comprises of ambience, tone, feelings, positive perception for training program, etc. Therefore, when the climate is favorable nothing goes wrong but when the climate is unfavorable, almost everything goes wrong.
- **Trainees' Learning Style:** the learning style, age, experience, educational background of trainees must be kept in mind in order to get the right pitch to the design of the program.
- **Training Strategies:** Once the training objective has been identified, the trainer translates it into specific training areas and modules. The trainer prepares the priority list of about what must be included, what could be excluded.

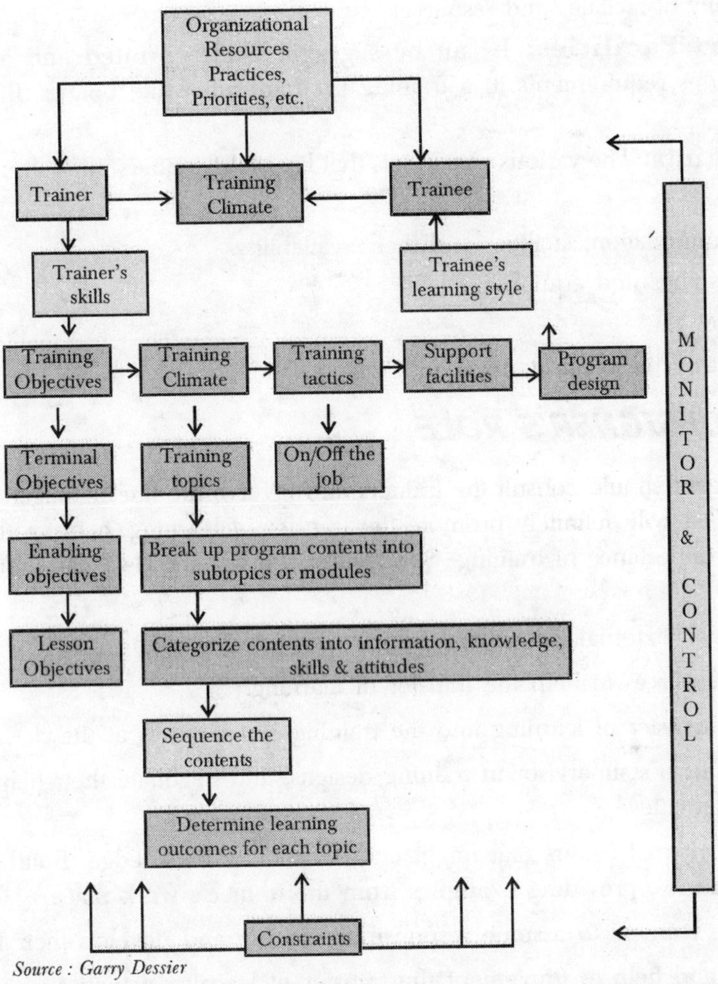

Source : Garry Dessier

- **Training Topics:** After formulating a strategy, trainer decides upon the content to be delivered. Trainers break the content into headings, topics, and modules. These topics and modules are then classified into information, knowledge, skills, and attitudes.
- **Training Tactics:** Once the objectives and the strategy of the training program becomes clear, trainer comes in the position to select most appropriate tactics or methods or techniques. The method selection depends on the following factors:
- Trainees' background
- Time allocated
- Style preference of trainer

- Level of competence of trainer
- Availability of facilities and resources, etc
- **Support Facilities:** It can be segregated into printed and audio visual aids. The various requirements in a training program are white boards, flip charts, markers, etc.
- **Constraints:** The various constraints that lay in the trainers mind are:
    - Time
    - Accommodation, facilities and their availability
    - Furnishings and equipments
    - Budget
    - Design of the training, etc

TRAINING DESIGNER'S ROLE

The training designer should consult the trainers and involve the line managers in the process of training design. This will definitely promote the transfer of learning, achieve the business goals, and enhance the importance of training. Specifically, the training designer should try to achieve the following:

(*a*) Minimize all external factors that inhibit transfer of learning.

(*b*) Provide resources to help the transfer of learning.

(*c*) Build the transfer of learning into the training programmes at the design stage.

(*d*) Involve learner's supervisor in training designs, and negotiate their help and support for training activities.

(*e*) Minimize internal factors that might limit transfer of knowledge. Build job-related issues into all courses, providing examples from the trainee's work place.

(*f*) Encourage learners to assume responsibility to use and develop their learning.

(*g*) Organize and help to implement the transfer of learning activities.

(*h*) Monitor the implementation of transfer of learning activities

Training Design Process

A process is a set of interrelated activities. Training, as a process, needs certain steps. The parties involved in the training are the learners, the trainers, the training organisation, and the organisation requiring training. The process of developing a training programme includes awareness of the need, checking with the client, and stipulating the symptoms.

• AWARENESS OF THE NEED

Organizations must ensure that the personnel are aware of the relevance and importance of their activities and how they contribute to the achievement of the quality objectives. Training manifests its importance for rising awareness of the personnel. Unless they know the worth of their contribution to the organisation, the relevance and importance of what they are doing, the consequence of performing an activity erroneously, and failure to achieve the desired target, it will be difficult to achieve business goals.

• CHECKING WITH THE CLIENT

An individual can comprehend his/her shortcomings, identifying the training needs, and the approach for the same and also the efforts. Excessive waste and scrap, deviation from the product specification, frequent breakdown of the machine an operator is working on, queuing of semi-finished components at the workstation, delays in processing and sending to the next workstation are only a few examples from the product layout system in manufacturing organisations. The client is the person, irrespective of whether he/she is the individual or the supervisor, who proposed the training needs. It is of immense importance to go back to the client for diagnosis and for probing the exact need to collect as many details as possible.

• STIPULATING THE SYMPTOMS

Suppose you have assigned a new task to an employee that he/she has not preformed earlier. This assignment may need completely new training. The task needs a different set of competency. The task of competency mapping might have been completed earlier, and the employee may not have all the competencies required to carry out the activities. Otherwise, the symptoms might be revealed from the standard of performance. To ensure that a training programme offers an integrated learning experience leading to the desired individual performance, you have to build-in the transfer of learning opportunities from the beginning. Otherwise, there can be the risk of an unstructured approach on which the learner fails to recognize and apply the learning, which might result from programme activities. There is also the likelihood that training will be understood by both learners and their managers as been confined to the off-the-job parts of the programme only. The fewer opportunities there are to practice and build upon the knowledge and skill acquired throughout a training programme, the less effective is the training likely to be. Each training programme will allow a different range of transfer of learning opportunities to be used, depending upon the circumstances.

In order to overcome the difficulties in ensuring continuing opportunities for learners to apply, practice, and develop their knowledge and skills, you can help them by doing the following:

1. Obtaining management support for training, as reflected in the organisation's training policy, and commitment to provide integrated training – An unstructured training cannot eliminate resistance base upon the pressure of work, precedence of unsuccessful training, and associated cost.
2. Discussing with learners and their supervisors on their roles in the training programme and their responsibilities – learners should actively participate in the learning process. A passive participant does not gain from the programme. This allows line supervisor to

plan work allocation to accommodate the follow-up activity. Discussions between a learner and his/her supervisors stabilize a 'psychological contract' for exploiting the learning opportunity.

3. Designing the transfer for learning opportunities to fit in with the aspirations and abilities of the learners and the supervisors – Consultation with both will help in deciding the most useful transfer of learning mechanism. This should result in the design of an effective training programme.
4. The effective transfer of learning from an off-the-job training course to the job situation obviously requires the content of the course to be based on an accurate identification of needs. During training design, you should preferably involve the line managers as they happen to be the main stakeholders facilitating the transfer of learning to the workplace.

Trainees & Trainers

TRAINEE

The trainee is a major stakeholder in a training program. The whole training program is developed for the trainees only. Each candidate plays an important role in the transfer of training because one participant's attitude regarding the training influence the other participants and also each participant can assist by advancing the learning process to realize the training objectives.

Participant's willingness to invest in the program is directly proportional to the benefits of the learning that the trainee could expect. Each participant forms their own perception towards training. Some perceptions remain the same during the program, while some faded depending upon the assessment of a program by the participant.

Some personnel factors that affect the trainee's learning are:

§ Family Situation

§ Personal Problems

§ Relation between the training program and personnel objective

§ Level of self esteem

§ Benefits expected from training

§ Comfort level with the trainer

§ Learning style of trainee

§ KSA of trainee

§ Previous training experiences

§ Desire for professional growth and development

Some environmental factors that affect the trainee's learning are:

§ Relationship with colleagues and subordinates
§ Training team
§ Trainer team
§ Training objective
§ Content of training
§ Training design i.e. methods, techniques, and strategies
§ Environment in the program
§ Composition of training group
§ Infrastructure i.e. eating facilities, tea/coffee breaks

No matter how good the training program is, in the end it is the participant only who decides whether to change his behavior or not. Trainees do not change their behavior merely because someone tells them to do. They change when they feel there is a need of it. They do it with their own learning style. The trainer and the organization can only try to remove the mental blocks of the trainee, rest depends on trainee itself.

TRAINERS

The effective transfer of training depends a lot on the trainer because it is the trainer only who can remove the mental block of trainee, motivate the trainee to learn, delete the negative perception of the trainee regarding the training. Besides all that, a lot depends on personnelity of trainer also.

The major competencies that are required to be present in a trainer are:

§ Presentation Skills
§ Business Skills i.e. budgeting, time management, negotiation, etc.
§ Content Development i.e. material production, graphics, layouts, etc
§ Self development
§ Interpersonnel skills
§ Good listening skills
§ Flexibility
§ Accepting the share of accountability, etc

Role of Trainer

§ **Assessing training needs to individuals:** The first and the most important task of a trainer is to access the training needs of trainees.

§ **Designing training programmes:** The next task of a trainer is to accurately design the training programme as per the needs of the individuals.

§ **Planning and coordinating the resources required:** The trainer next has to plan and coordinate the resources.

§ **Evaluating the training programme:** Further the trainer has to evaluate the training programme to check its effectiveness.

§ **Administration and record keeping:** Lastly the trainer administers and keeps the records of the training programme for the future requirements and feedback.

Role of Trainers

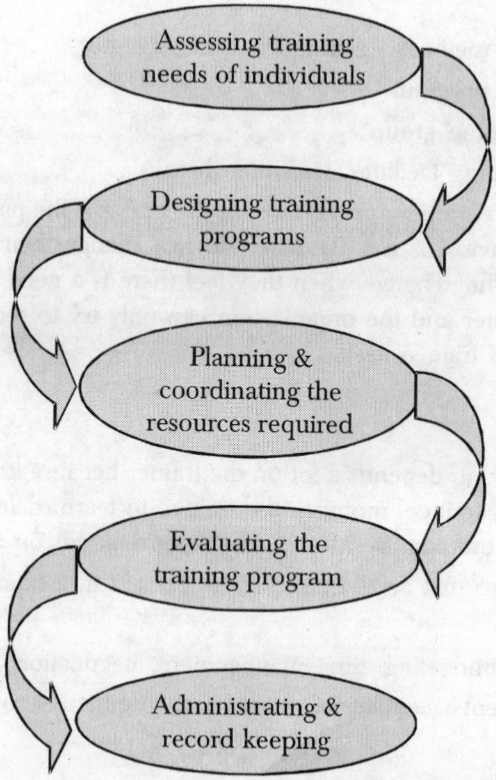

Case Study

1. SALES TRAINING AT ABC COMPANY

Few years ago, ABC Company developed a training strategy for training its global sales force. An important feature of the strategy was to create a master training plan for each year. The organization's strategic plans, objectives, and functional tactics would drive this plan. Once an initial procedure was designed it was then evaluated and critiqued by the top management, different units, and training council. The input from these stakeholders would be summarized and transferred into a master training plan.

The major question that was asked by the designers of training program was, "what results do we want from salespeople after the training program is over?" Answer to this question becomes the objective of the training program.

Then training content was designed, videos were made. The videos took 3 to 6 months to produce. Video contains live production plants, clients' offices, partner offices, suppliers, manufacturers' locations, and other locations. Videos were used to train sales people in various areas, such as:

Market information i.e. about customer profile, market updates, and computer integrated manufacturing applications, etc

Sales Process i.e. how to deal in the situation of conflicts with customer, coaching on undesirable behavior, supplement skills developed during live courses

Product information, such as, product usage, applications, system description, product description, comparison with competitor's products, etc

Policies and procedures, i.e. about sales contests, incentive plans on achieving targets, annual bonuses, winners receiving the best salesperson award to motivate the sales force

Around thousands of sales persons were getting a specific video training. The sales people were getting training material along with the video. Sales representatives then watch video, follow the directions, and refer to the material if faces any problem. When salespeople feel they have mastered the material, they would take an exam and call a toll-free number to transmit responses to exam.

Salespeople who successfully passed an exam were factored into performance and merit reviews as well as promotional opportunities. Those who couldn't pass the exam were asked to go through the material and video again before retaking the exam. If the salesperson failed an exam again, the reporting manager was notified.

This case gives rise to few important questions. These questions are:

1. In today's technological world, is video still the best way to deliver the training?
2. Is video the most effective way to achieve training objectives?

2. COAL INDIA LTD.

Human Resource Development in Coal India.

The human resource development functions in Coal India have been set up to deal with the development of existing human resources as well as to look ahead with a clear perspective on technological advances and growth of manpower to fulfill the demands of production.

Technical Training

Technical training is conducted to provide knowledge regarding the technology being used in each subsidiary and any other technology being conceived at the corporate level for which preparedness is necessary to meet the current shortage of skilled manpower and also preparing statutory personnel for meeting statutory obligation through training. In order to implement the above, workers are exposed to:

- **Basic Course:** This is appropriate to technology, equipment and system
- **Refresher Course:** This is taught once in three years to those who have already working in a specific skill area.
- **Specialized Course:** In case of change technology, in equipment configuration and capacity and improvement in the system of production, suitable inputs are given to all the new entrants to the critical-skill areas.

Management Training

A need-based training is imparted to executives at each level and at the time of assuming the charge at the new position, i.e., entry to the higher level, at the Management Training Centre of each subsidiary companies for the level from E1 to E5 and at the Apex Training Centre, Indian Institute of Coal Management, Ranchi for higher level executives, i.e., from M1 to M3 level

Transformation training

This is a planned attempt to help those who join CIL as part of he management policy and for the workmen who are required to acquire skills to move from conventional to semi-mechanized minds with intermediate technology or at the instance of closure of minds and surplus manpower. These trainees are used as source of supply of manpower in critical and non-critical areas of skills for the technology specific to the subsidiary company.

General Development Training

When there is a change in the scenario with reference to the status of a mine, specifically in ECL, BCCL and, to an extent CCL, and separate focus for MCL, NCL, SECL, and WCL, knowledge about the vision of the company, the financial status of the organisation, the criteria for raising productivity, cost parameters, criteria for excellence in performance, etc. is imparted through intra-organisational communication as well as face-to-face interaction with the workers and supervisors in a planned way. This is called general development training.

Q.1 Training should be need based". Comment.

Summary

This chapter begins with the introduction to setting of training objectives which form an important part of training programmes; it further provides a detailed knowledge of training methods and techniques which are helpful in training the employees. This chapter also throws light on how the training programmes should be designed and also the role of trainers and trainees is emphasized.

Concept Review Questions

OBJECTIVES

1. Training _________assist trainers to design the training program.
2. Generally line managers ask the personnel manager to formulate the training _________.
3. The _________method requires skilled trainers
4. Each apprentice is given a programme of _________according to a predetermined schedule.
5. _________refers to moving employees from job to job to another.
6. Under the _________, group of trainees are given and asked to solve an actual organizational problem.
7. _________ is a technique that duplicates as nearly as possible the actual conditions encountered on the job.
8. _________ training utilizes equipment which closely resembles the actual ones used on the job.

(objectives, policies, JIT, assignments, Job rotation, Committee Assignments, Simulation, vestibule)

SHORT QUESTIONS

1. What are training objectives?
2. Mention any two objectives of training.
3. What is employee training?
4. How is on-the-job training different from of-the-job-training?
5. What is job instruction training?
6. What is job rotation?
7. What is apprenticeship training?
8. What is coaching?
9. What are committee assignments?

10. Explain simulation training.
11. What do mean by vestibule training?
12. What do mean by role playing?
13. How is role playing different from case study method of training?
14. How are audio-visual aids helpful in training employees?
15. What is the importance of conference method of training?
16. What is the importance of designing a training program?
17. What are the principles that should be kept in mind while designing a sound employee training program?
18. What are the personnel factors that affect the learning of the trainees?
19. What are the environmental factors that affect the learning of the trainees?
20. What is the role of trainers in the training program?
21. What are the major competencies required in a trainer to be effective?
22. Which training technique would you suggest for each of the following occupations? Why?
    (*a*) A clerk in an office
    (*b*) A welder
    (*c*) An assembly-line worker
    (*d*) An inexperienced supervisor

LONG QUESTIONS

1. What are the important objectives of training?
2. Why do you feel setting objectives of training accurately is important?
3. What is employee training? Explain the important techniques of training?
4. What are the different methods of training on the basis of on-the-job and off-the-job training?
5. What is job rotation? How does it help in acquiring new skills and knowledge?
6. What is apprenticeship training? What are its advantages and disadvantages?
7. What is coaching? Define its merits and demerits?
8. What are committee assignments and how are they helpful in training employees?
9. Explain simulation training. What are its components?
10. What do mean by vestibule training? What are its benefits?
11. What do mean by role playing and what are its advantages and disadvantages?

12. Differentiate between the lecture method of training and seminars or discussions.
13. How is sensitivity training an important part of the training methods?
14. Write in detail the steps required in designing a training program.
15. What is the role of trainees in training program?
16. "Training programs are helpful to avoid personnel obsolescence." Discuss

4

Role of Training

TRAINING FOR SPECIAL GROUPS

It is the responsibility of the organizations to provide training in various areas and upgrade its employees. Organizations provide training to their employees in the following areas:

1. **Company Policies and Procedure/ Induction Training:** This area of training is to be provided with a view to acquainting the new employee with the company rule, practices, procedures, tradition, management, organisation structure, environment product/ services offered by the company etc. This acquaintance enables the new employee to adjust himself with the changing situations. Information regarding company rules and policies creates favorable attitudes of confidence in the minds of new employee about the company and its products/services, as well as it develops in him a sense of respect for the existing employees of the company and the like. The company also provides the first hand information to the employees about the skills needed by the company and its development programmes, Quality of products/services and the like. This enables the new employees to know his share of contribution to the organisation's growth and development.
2. **Training in Specific Skills:** This area of training is to enable the employee more effective on the job. The trainer trains the employee regarding various skills necessary to do the actual job. For e.g., the clerk in the bank should be trained in the skill of making entries correctly and arithmetic calculations, quick comparison of figures, entries and the like. Similarly the technical officers are to be trained in the skills of project appraisal, supervision, follow up and the like.
3. **Human Relations Training:** Human Relation training assumes greater significance in organisations as employees have to maintain human relations not only with other employees but also with their customers. Employees are to be trained in the areas of self-learning, interpersonal competence, group dynamics, perception, leadership styles, motivation, grievance redressal, disciplinary procedures etc. This training enables the employees for better teamwork, which leads to improved efficiency and productivity of

the organisation.

4. **Problem Solving Training/Remedial Training:** Most of the organizational problems are common to the employees dealing the same activity at different levels of the oragnisation. Further some of the problems of different managers may have the same root cause. Hence, management may call together all managerial personal to discuss common problems so as to arrive at effective solutions across the table. This not only helps in solving the problems but also serves as a forum for the exchange of ideas and information that could be utilized. The trainer has to organize such meetings, train and encourage the trainees to participate actively in such meetings.
5. **Managerial And Supervisory Training:** Even the non-managers sometimes perform managerial and supervisory functions like planning, decision making, organizing, maintaining interpersonal relations, directing and controlling. Hence, management has to train the employees in managerial and supervisory skills also.
6. **Apprentice Training:** The Apprentice Act, 1961 requires industrial units of specified industries to provide training in basic skills and knowledge in specified trades to uneducated employees/apprentices with a view to improving their employment opportunities or to enable them to start their own industry. This type of training generally ranges between one year to four years. This training is generally used for providing technical knowledge in the areas like trades, crafts etc.

EXECUTIVE / MANAGEMENT DEVELOPMENT PROGRAMMES

What is Executive/Management Development?

Today, it is the growth that makes one person stay at the company. The opportunity and challenges is what keeps a person satisfied and charmed with his job. Companies have understood this fact and therefore are forming policies and procedures to develop their employees.

Executive development Program (EDP) is one such program. With Human resource making a move from a welfare department to a strategic partner, more and more companies are undertaking this program.

Executive/Management development is a systematic process of growth and development by which the managers develop their abilities to manage. So it is the result of not only participants in formal courses of instruction but also of actual job experience. It is concerned with improving the performance of the Managers by giving them opportunities for growth and development. There are four major steps to be covered during the EDP-

1. **Problem Assessment:** the experts along with the concerned employees and CEO shall begin with an assessment of the company's current problem and owner's plans of the future.
2. **Management Audit and Appraisal:** there shall be regular feedback sessions to check as to whether we are reaching where we are supposed to reach.

3. **Analysis of Development Needs:** here the problem that has been uncovered shall be tried to and remedied via a development program.
4. **Identify Replacement needs:** the assessment may uncover a need to recruit and select new management talent. The format of EDP will vary with company's size and nature of operation so as to provide optimum result.

Managerial effectiveness has an enormous impact on a firm's success. Therefore, companies must provide instruction for managers and high-potential management candidates in order to help them perform current and future jobs with the utmost proficiency. Management development has long been an important component of corporate strategic planning. In fact, many companies consider the identification and development of next-generation managers to be their top human resource challenge.

Management development is important for new managers because these individuals really need instruction on how to perform their new supervisory jobs. Even so, companies often allow employees to make the transition to management with little or no training, leaving them with feelings of frustration, inadequacy, and dismay. More experienced managers also benefit from management development. A majority of first-line managers have their sights set on higher-level management jobs. Given these ambitions, companies need to provide lower-level and mid-level managers with formal development programs in order to help them climb the corporate ladder.

Management instruction programs should bridge gaps between what individuals already know and what they need to know for their new positions. Managers need different skills at each managerial level. The instructional programs needed to produce these skills are as follows:

Instructional Needs at Different Managerial Levels

First-line managers need training in

- Basic supervision
- Motivation
- Career planning
- Performance feedback

Middle managers need training in

- Designing and implementing effective group and intergroup work and information systems
- Defining and monitoring group-level performance indicators
- Diagnosing and resolving problems within and among work groups
- Designing and implementing reward systems that support cooperative behavior

Executives need training in

- Broadening their understanding of how factors such as competition, world economies, politics, and social trends influence the effectiveness of the organization

A variety of approaches are used to teach these subjects. Some are in traditional classroom-type settings, while others are taught outside of the classroom via career resource centers, job rotation, mentoring, and special projects.

Steps in Management/Executive Development

1. **Ascertaining development needs:** The organization at the time of planning, should know; what types of managers are required to meet his present requirements and its future needs, taking into consideration the anticipated changes in production methods and techniques, in the industrial development of the country and in the size of the organization. It should also be decided how many vacancies are to be filled in by the process of promotion. The management must provide the opportunities for the development of the talent and capabilities of its present employees to meet the challenges of the higher jobs.
2. **Appraisal of the Present Management Talent:** After ascertaining the needs of the development, the management should appraise the talent of its present staff by comparing the actual performance with the standard performance. How to develop a person, can be judged only by evaluating his performance on various occasions in performing his managerial duties.
3. **Inventory of management Manpower:** An inventory of qualified personnel should be prepared and a selection for the various development programmes should be made. Such inventory will provide all necessary personnel data regarding the individuals qualified for development.
4. **Individual development programme:** The chief executive must know the limitations of the individual and chalk out the various development plans according to their mental and physical characteristics.
5. **Establishment of Training and development Programme:** As far as possible, a systematic procedure should be introduced for the development of executives. Crash programme may be used for the purpose which includes development programmes in the fields of human relations creativity, training, leadership capacity etc.

TECHNIQUES OF EXECUTIVE/ MANAGEMENT DEVELOPMENT

Classroom Instruction

Classroom training takes place within the organization or outside at seminars and universities. The subjects typically covered in these programs are briefly described as follows:

Content Areas of Classroom Instruction

- **Job Duties and Responsibilities.** Trainees learn what they must do to fulfill the company's expectations of them.

- **Policies and Procedures.** Trainees learn company policies and procedures.
- **Employee Familiarization.** Trainees become familiar with the job functions of their employees. The training provides specific instructions on how to review job descriptions, performance standards, personnel files, and so forth.
- **Attitudes and Confidence**. The training attempts to establish new attitudes toward the job employees, and the manager, and to build the confidence necessary for managers to be effective on the job.
- **Handling Employee Interactions.** Trainees are taught how to handle interpersonal problems effectively through such techniques as behavior modelling.
- **Career Development.** Trainees learn about career opportunities in higher levels of management and how they may advance in the future.
- **General Management Training.** These courses typically cover Labour relations, management theory and practice, labor economics, and general management functions.
- **Human Relations/Leadership Programs**. These topics are narrower than general management programs. They focus on the human relations problems of leadership, supervision, attitude toward employees, and communication.
- **Self-Awareness Program.** The content of these programs understands one's own behavior and how that behavior is viewed by others, identifying the so-called games people play, and learning about one's strengths and weaknesses.
- **Problem-Solving/Decision-Making Programs.** The emphasis is on teaching generalized problem-solving and decision-making skills that would be applicable to the wide range of work problems that managers encounter.

Lecture

Most training experts criticize lectures because they are passive learning devices, focusing on one-way communication to learners who do not have the opportunity to clarify material. Lectures generally fail to gain and maintain learner's attention unless they are given by someone who is able to make the material meaningful and promote questions and discussions. Lectures are most appropriate for situations where simple knowledge acquisition is the goal (e.g., describing company history during a new employee orientation session).However; lectures are not well suited to serve as the sole training method for teaching management skills, because the format does not provide trainees with feedback or the opportunity for practice.

Case Method

As the name suggests, the case method requires management trainees to analyze cases or scenarios depicting realistic job situations. Cases often are structured like a play that opens in the middle of a story and uses flashbacks to describe the action that lead up to the opening scene, where an employee has just made a key decision. The rest of the case lays out the documentation and data available to the decision maker at the time of the decision. Questions are posed at the end of the case that asks the trainees to analyze the situation and recommend a solution. For instance, they may be asked to state the nature of the problem, identify the events that led to the problem, and indicate what the individual should do to resolve the problem.

The case method rests on the assumption that people are most likely to retain and use what they learn if they reach an understanding through "guided discovery." Trainers act as guides or facilitators. Cases typically do not have right or wrong answers. Therefore, the aim of the method is not to teach trainees the "right" answer, but rather to teach them how to identify potential problems and recommend realistic actions.

Critics of this method talk at the lack of direction trainees receive when analyzing a case. What if they arrive at a poor decision? Moreover, trainees do not get the opportunity to practice their skills. For instance, after analyzing a case involving a subordinate who has repeatedly arrived at work late, the trainees may conclude that the manager should have said something sooner and must now provide counselling. However, the case method does not afford trainees the opportunity to practice their counselling skills.

Role-Playing

As an instructional technique, role-playing presents a hypothetical problem involving human interaction. Trainees spontaneously act out that interaction face-to-face. Participants are then given feedback by the trainer and the rest of the group on their performance so they may gain insight regarding the impact of their behavior on others. The issues addressed during feedback typically revolve around these types of questions:

What was correct about the participant's behavior?

What was incorrect about the participant's behavior?

How did the participant's behavior make the other participants feel?

How could the trainee have handled the situation more effectively?

Role-playing may be used to develop skills in any area that involves human interaction. The method is most often used for teaching human relations skills and sales techniques. Role-playing provides management trainees with an opportunity to practice the skill being taught. It thus goes beyond the case method, which merely requires the trainee to make a decision regarding how to handle a situation. These two methods are often used in conjunction with one another. That is, after analyzing a case and recommending a solution, trainees are asked to act out the solution in the form of a role-play.

Critics of the role-playing method point out those role-players who are often given little guidance beforehand on how to handle transactions. This may cause them to make mistakes, resulting in embarrassment and a loss of self-confidence. When their mistake-ridden role-play is finished, they sit, never getting the opportunity to do it correctly.

Behavior Modeling

Behavior modeling is based on the idea that workers learn best when they see how a task should be performed and then practice the task with feedback until they are competent. This method is similar to role-playing in that the trainees act out situations playing certain roles. However, the methods differ in two important ways. First, behavior modelling teaches trainees a preferred way to perform a task. Second, the interactions occurring during behavior modeling are practice sessions, not role plays. The trainees practice only the right way. If they make a mistake, the trainer immediately corrects them and asks them to repeat the step correctly.

A behavior modeling program typically consists of the following steps:

- **Present An Overview Of The Material:** This usually consists of a brief lecture that describes training objectives and the importance of the skill to be learned.
- **Describe The Procedural Steps:** The trainee learns the one best way (or at least an effective way) to handle a situation. Case and role-playing methods, on the other hand, stress the variety of effective ways to handle a situation and do not emphasize any one particular approach.
- **Model Or Demonstrate The Procedural Steps:** The trainee is shown a "model" of how the task is to be performed correctly. The model usually is presented in the form of a videotape or live demonstration.
- **Allow Guided Practice:** Trainees then practice the modeled behaviors. As previously stated, these sessions are similar to role-plays, except that trainees are given feedback by the instructor (or classmates) during the skill practice session, rather than after. This procedure forces trainees to correct mistakes as soon as they are made, assuring them an opportunity to practice the correct way of performing the task. Practice sessions start with simple problems, similar to those depicted in the model. Later practice sessions are made more realistic by adding complexity to the situation.
- **Provide On-The-Job Reinforcement:** Participants' managers often go through identical training programs to ensure that they will understand what their employees are learning and, hence, support these new behaviors back on the job.
- **Behavior Modeling Has Become Very Popular:** Research examining its effectiveness has been quite favourable. Behavior modeling works because it successfully incorporates each of the aforementioned learning principles: it captures and maintains trainees' attention and provides ample opportunity for practice and feedback.

Non-Classroom Methods

Non-classroom methods include career resource centers, job rotation, coaching and mentoring, and special assignments.

Career Resource Centers

Some organizations make learning opportunities available to interested candidates by establishing career resource centers, which usually include an in-house library with relevant reading material.

In some companies, candidates simply are given recommended readings lists. Other companies provide management candidates with comprehensive career-planning guides that contain company-related information about available resources, career options, and counselling contacts. These individuals also may be given workbooks that provide written assignments.

Job Rotation

Job rotation exposes management trainees to various organizational settings by rotating them through a number of departments. Thus, trainees have an opportunity to gain an overall perspective of the organization and learn how various parts interrelate. Additionally, they face new challenges during these assignments that may foster new skill development. Trainees usually have full management responsibility during these assignments. For example, in one hospital new department supervisors rotate through all major departments on a monthly basis, serving in a managerial capacity during their "tours." Although they often learn a lot from such training, they also may make harmful mistakes during their learning period because they lack knowledge of the functional area that they are supervising.

COACHING AND MENTORING

Coaching is a method of management development that is conducted on the job, in which experienced managers or peers advise and guide trainees in solving managerial problems. Typically, less experienced managers are coached by their direct supervisor or a co-worker on their specific performance of managerial tasks. An upper-level manager is likely to coach several lower-level managers at once, offering feedback, helping them to find expert advice, and providing resources.

Under this technique, the superior coaches the job knowledge and skill, to his subordinates. He briefs the trainees what is expected of them and guides how to get it. He also watches their performance and directs them to correct the mistakes. The main objective of this training is to provide them diversified knowledge. Coaching is recognized as one of the managerial responsibilities, and the manger as an obligation to train and develop the subordinates working under him. He delegates his authority to the subordinates to prepare them to handle the complex situations.

Mentoring is different from coaching in several ways. Mentors are experienced supervisors who establish close, one-on-one relationships with new managers, called protégés. A mentor usually is someone two or three levels higher in the organization than the protégé who teaches, guides, advises, counsels, and serves as a role model; the mentor is not necessarily the protégé's direct supervisor. Mentoring can help the protégé to form common values with the organization's senior leadership and better understand his or her role in the company. Additionally, protégés are often advocated for and protected by a mentor. A mentor may ensure that the protégé is assigned high-visibility projects, or even change negative opinions about the protégé that may be held by others in the company. While a coach focuses on job-specific advice, a mentor is likely to give advice on a broader range of topics related to the protégé's career success.

SPECIAL ASSIGNMENT

Companies sometimes assign special, non-routine job duties to trainees in order to prepare them for future assignments. One such special project is called action learning, which derives its name from the fact that the trainees can learn by doing. Candidates are given real problems generated by management. Trainees might be given a written assignment that specifies objectives, action plans, target dates, and the name of the person responsible for monitoring the completion of the assignment. For instance, trainees might be asked to study the company's budgeting procedures and submit a written critique.

Another type of special project is the task force, where trainees are grouped together and asked to tackle an actual organizational problem. For example, the task force may be asked to develop a new performance appraisal form, solve a quality problem, or design a program to train new employees. Trainees not only gain valuable experience by serving on a task force, they also have the opportunity to "show their stuff" to others within the organization.

MANAGEMENT SUCCESSION PLANNING

Most organizations base their management development and training efforts on succession planning, a systematic process of defining future management requirements and identifying the candidates who best meet them. Unfortunately, many companies take a very informal approach to succession planning. Identification of high-potential candidates is largely subjective, based on the opinions of the nominating managers, who choose "fast-track" or "superstar" employees with little consideration of the actual requirements of future positions. Research has found that promotions within the management ranks are often based on employee behaviors that have no bearing on managerial effectiveness; specifically, networking had the greatest influence on managerial promotions, even though networking made no contribution to actual performance. Additionally, ill-conceived succession planning activities can have disastrous consequences; as many as 30 percent of all newly placed executives are unprepared for their jobs and ultimately fail to meet company expectations.

Elements of an effective succession planning program involve human resource planning, defining qualifications for positions, identifying career paths, and developing replacement charts. The first step in succession planning is human resource planning, in which forecasting is used to determine projected staffing needs for the next several years. Based on these needs, management succession plans should specify key management positions for which staffing should be targeted. Succession plans should next define pertinent individual qualifications needed for each targeted position, which are based on information derived from a job analysis. A firm then identifies individuals with high potential for promotion into or through the management ranks. This is accomplished by assessing employee abilities and career interests through records of career progress, experience, past performance, and self-reported interests regarding future career steps.

Following the above steps, an organization identifies a career path for each high-potential candidate (i.e., those who have the interest and ability to move upward in the organization). A career path typically appears as a flow chart, indicating the sequencing of specific jobs that may lead one up the organizational ladder to a targeted job. The final step is to develop replacement charts that indicate the availability of candidates and their readiness to step into the various management positions. Such charts usually are depicted as diagrams superimposed onto the organizational chart. These show possible replacement candidates, in rank order, for each management position. Rank orders are often based on the candidates' "overall potential scores," derived on the basis of their past performance, experience, test scores, and so on.

Managements Games

It is a classroom exercise, in which teams of students compete against each other to achieve common objective. The game is designed to be a close representation of real life conditions. The trainees are asked to make decisions about production, cost, research and development, etc., for an organization. Since they are often divided into teams as competing companies, experience is obtained in team work. Under this method, the trainees learn by analyzing problems by using some intention and by making trial and error type of decisions. Any wrong is corrected by the trainer or sometimes a second chance is given to do something all over again.

Syndicate Method Under this method, 5 or 6 groups consisting of about 10 members are formed. Each group (Syndicate) is composed of carefully selected men who, on the one and, represents fair cross section of the executive life of the country, i.e. men from public sector and private sector Undertakings, civil and defense services, banking, insurance, etc., and on the other hand, a good well balance team of management from different fields, i.e., production, marketing, personnel, finance, etc. The groups are given assignments, made up before hand to be submitted within a specified date and time. Each man in the group is appointed leader of the group for the performance of the given task by rotation and so for the secretary for the subdivision of the course. Each task is assigned in the form of a 'Brief', a document prepared by the experts on the faculty with meticulous care. It also fixes the time by which the study is to be completed. Lectures by experts are also arranged to supplement the study. The report prepared are submitted by a group is circulated among the members of the other groups for comparative study and critical evaluation. The leader or chairman of the group is required to present the views of his group in the joint session and justify his group's view in case of criticism or questions.

Sensitivity Training or T-Group

In sensitivity training, the executives spends about two work-hours attending the lectures on the subject such as leadership and communication. The members, under this method, sit around a table and discuss. The trainer, usually a psychologist, neither leads the discussion nor suggests what should be discussed but only guides the discussion. The members freely discuss and criticize the behavior of each other thereby giving a feed back positive or negative.

Programmed Instruction

Programmed instruction as gained a lot of importance both in training and in industry in modern times it includes teaching machines, automatic instruction and programmed learning. It is an application of science of learning to the task of training and education. The core feature of programmed instruction is the participation by the trainee and immediate feedback by him. Programmed instruction machines include films, tapes, programmed books, illustrations, printed material, diagrams, etc. it performs two functions: - (i) provides information to the learner, and (ii) provides feed back whether the response is correct or wrong.

Selective Readings

Many executives find it very difficult to do much reading other than that absolutely required in the performance of their jobs. Some organizations provide some time for reading which will advance the general knowledge and background of the individuals. Many organizations purchase some high level journals like the Commerce, the Capitalist, the Management in Govt., etc. And dailies like the Economic Times, the Financial Express, etc.

Johari Window

A **Johari window** is a cognitive psychological tool created by **Joseph Luft and Harry Ingham in 1955** in the United States, used to help people better understand their interpersonal communication and relationships. It is used primarily in self-help groups and corporate settings as a heuristic exercise.

Johari Window

	known to self	Not known to self
Known to others	Arena	Blind Spot
Not known to others	Facade	Unknown

When performing the exercise, the subject is given a list of 55 adjectives and picks five or six that they feel describe their own personality. Peers of the subject are then given the same list, and each pick five or six adjectives that describe the subject. These adjectives are then mapped onto a grid. **Charles Handy** calls this concept the Johari House with four rooms. Room 1 is the part of ourselves that we see and others see. Room 2 is the aspect that others see but we are not aware of. Room 3 is the most mysterious room in that the unconscious or subconscious bit of us is seen by neither ourselves nor others. Room 4 is our private space, which we know but keep from others.

Managerial Grid Model

The **managerial grid model** (1964) is a behavioral leadership model developed by **Robert Blake and Jane Mouton**. This model originally identified five different leadership styles based on the *Concern for people* and the *Concern for production*. The optimal leadership style in this model is based on Theory Y.

The model

The model is represented as a grid with *concern for production* as the X-axis and *concern for people* as the Y-axis; each axis ranges from 1 (Low) to 9 (High). The resulting leadership styles are as follows:

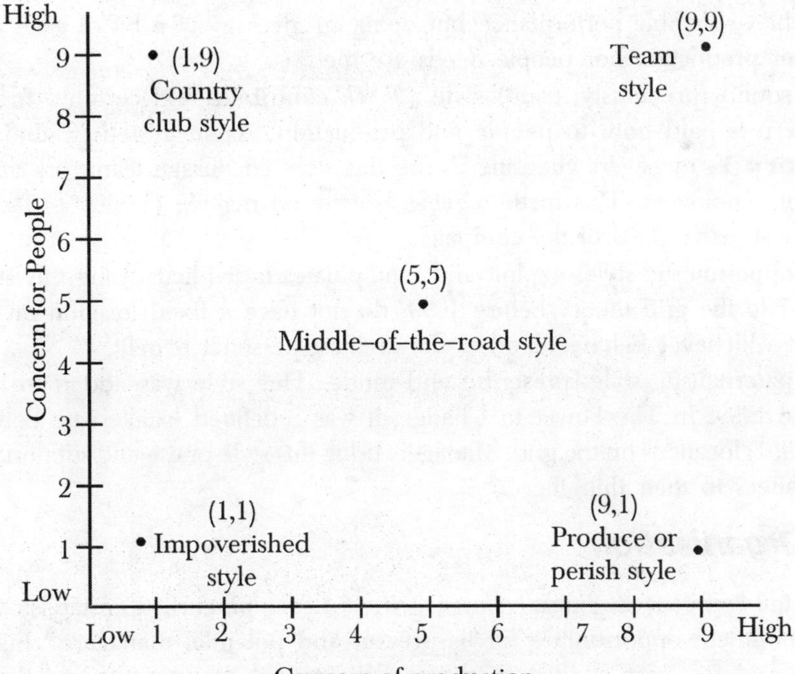

· The indifferent (previously called impoverished) style (1, 1): evade and elude. In this style, managers have low concern for both people and production. Managers use this style to preserve job and job seniority, protecting themselves by avoiding getting into trouble. The main concern for the manager is not to be held responsible for any mistakes, which results in less innovative decisions.

- The accommodating (previously, country club) style (1, 9): yield and comply. This style has a high concern for people and a low concern for production. Managers using this style pay much attention to the security and comfort of the employees, in hopes that this will increase -performance. The resulting atmosphere is usually friendly, but not necessarily very productive.
- The dictatorial (previously, produce or perish) style (9, 1): control and dominate. With a high concern for production, and a low concern for people, managers using this style find employee needs unimportant; they provide their employees with money and expect performance in return. Managers using this style also pressure their employees through rules and punishments to achieve the company goals. This dictatorial style is based on Theory X of **Douglas McGregor**, and is commonly applied by companies on the edge of real or perceived failure. This style is often used in case of crisis management.
- The status quo (previously, middle-of-the-road) style (5, 5): balance and compromise. Managers using this style try to balance between company goals and workers' needs. By giving some concern to both people and production, managers who use this style hope to achieve suitable performance but doing so gives away a bit of each concern so that neither production nor people needs are met.
- The sound (previously, team) style *(9, 9)*: contribute and commit. In this style, high concern is paid both to people and production. As suggested by the propositions of **Theory Y**, managers choosing to use this style encourage teamwork and commitment among employees. This method relies heavily on making employees feel themselves to be constructive parts of the company.
- The opportunistic style: exploit and manipulate. Individuals using this style, which was added to the grid theory before 1999, do not have a fixed location on the grid. They adopt whichever behaviour offers the greatest personal benefit.
- The paternalistic style: prescribe and guide. This style was added to the grid theory before 1999. In The Power to Change, it was redefined to alternate between the (1, 9) and (9, 1) locations on the grid. Managers using this style praise and support, but discourage challenges to their thinking.

Role of Organisation

"The role of the company in executive/management development is to establish the programme and the development opportunities for its present and potential managers." Just exposing the employees to lectures, case studies, readings, job rotation, assignments and the like does not guarantee that they will learn. What is more important is the effort of the individual. Each individual has to make his own contribution to the development of himself, as others can only create the opportunity. The saying **"We can take the horse to the water but we cannot make it drink"** cannot be forgotten here.

"Executive development is eventually something that the executive has to attain himself. But he will do this much better if he has been given encouragement, guidance and opportunity by his company." The role of the company is to provide conditions that accelerate the growth. And these conditions should be part of the organisational climate itself, in order to be away from the unrealistic expectation that we can create and develop managers only in class room.

Characteristics of Managers

The word manager has been used to mean people at different levels of hierarchy. To some, the term means only the top man at the top rung of the ladder. To others a manager is any person who supervises others. But in fact to be called a manager one neither has to be at the top of the organisation, nor should one necessarily supervise others. All those who perform all or some of the basic functions of management to some degree regularly or occasionally can be called managers.

Characteristics of a Manager are as follows:

1. He moves rapidly from job to job. It now takes 20 years on the average to rise from the first level manager to president, during which time there are seven geographical moves, 11 potential ones, and countless numbers of special and project assignments. More than before, the successful manager's career may include moving from one company to another.
2. He is flexible, realistic and sensitive to the complexities of his work environment. Compare with less successful mangers, he is both challenged, and comfortable in, situations filled with high risk and ambiguity.
3. He earns his spurs by handling critical assignments, which are more important than routine work done well.
4. Very often, he has a "sponsor", someone from the higher management who is impressed by his abilities, finds him useful to have around, and who looks after his interest. It helps if the sponsor is himself moving up rapidly.
5. He engages in "anticipatory socialization"; at each stage he occupies the values of those who are a step above him.
6. He is not necessarily an "organisation conformist". High level managers tend to be more "outer directed" and less concerned with pleasing others than are those at lower levels.
7. A manager should be skill full and knowledgeable, technical skills are less important whereas the conceptual skills are especially important at the top level. Human skills are important at all levels. It should also be remembered that, at the same level the skills required of a production executive differ from that of a marketing executive.

Though the success of the Executive/Management Development depends on the commitment of executives manager at all levels, its launching should be done by the chief of the organization, since it is a fundamental policy, decision that involves time, various resources and organizational efficiencies. Planning and administration of the programme may be handed over to a committee composed of a senior executive, while the day-to-day administration of the same can be performed by the personnel department.

Evolution of Executive/Management Development

Efficient and loyal workers were promoted to the supervisory of management positions and it was soon realized that "Supervisor workers do not necessarily make supervisor managers. This realization necessitated the need for planned programmes for the section, training and development of managerial personnel."

Formal management development programmes started emerging in the late 1940s and 1950s. Several forces have operated to cause the expansion of he management development activities. To name only a few –

1. Shift from owner managed to professional managed enterprises.
2. Management has been recognized as a distinct kind of occupation consisting of acquired scales and unified body of knowledge.

Objective of Executive/Management development programmes:

The executive/management development programmes are organized with a few to achieve specific objectives. They are:

1. To over haul the management machinery.
2. To improve the performance of the manager.
3. To give the specilization on overall view of the functions of an organization and equip them to co-ordinate each other's efforts effectively.
4. To identify the persons with the required potential and to prepare them for senior positions.
5. To increase the morale of the members of the management group.
6. To increase the versatility of the management group.
7. To keep the executives abreast with the changes and development in their respective fields.
8. To create the management succession which can take over in case of contingencies.
9. To improve thought process and analytical ability.
10. To broaden the outlook of the executives regarding his role position and responsibilities.
11. To understand the conceptual issues relating to economic, social and technical areas.
12. To understand the problems of human relations and improve human relation skills.
13. To stimulate creative thinking.

Achievement of the above stated objectives is very difficult as some factors inhibit the management development process.

Impediments to Executive/Management Development Pogrammes

1. Job security of the employees, its stability, and pension; these slow down the mobility of employees and check the recruitment of younger people;
2. Supervisors at different levels, especially in the middle management, often feel trapped. They are "frozen", i.e., there is little prospect of their promotion because of the limited opportunities for advancements available in an establishment.
3. Home ownership, home-sickness, close ties with one's family, community and social activities inhibit development to a large extent; and when these are accompanied by the absence of job security and changes of promotion, the employees tend to stress the non-job aspects of their lives.
4. Relations between supervisor and subordinates are often not conducive to management development when a subordinate is afraid of the work of the supervisor, or when no challenging situation are offered to him, the chances of his development are greatly reduced. The supervisor also finds little incentives for developing subordinates despite lip services, partly because he does not have much time for it, and partly because of his reluctance to promote subordinates lest he lose a good worker and may have to train fresh personnel of unknown quality.

Essential Ingredients of the Executive/Management Development Programmes

The essential ingredients of the management development programme can be explained through the step of management process.

The important steps of ingredients of a management development programmes are:

1. Analyzing of Organizations Present and Development Needs
2. Appraisal of Present Management Talent
3. Inventory of Management Manpower
4. Planning of Individual Development Programme
5. Establishment of Development Programme
6. Evaluation of the Programme

Pre-requisites for the Success Of Executive/Management Development Programmes

1. The top management should accept responsibility for getting the policy of development

executed. For this purpose, a senior officer may be placed in charge to initiate and implement the MDP /EDP (Management Development Programme/ Executive Development Programme).

2. Management/Executive Development is essentially a "line job". It takes place on the job and involves both the man and his boss.
3. Every manager must accept direct responsibility for developing managers under his control on the job, and a high priority should be given to his task.
4. Management/Executive development must be geared to the needs of the company and the individual.
5. A policy of promotion from within is necessary incentive for managers to develop an organization
6. Management development starts with the section of the right material for managerial ranks. It is essential to ensure that really good material is fed into the programme at the entry level.

In our view, the management development programme should be based on a definite strategy, which should spell out the type, coverage and objective of the programme. The multitier supervisory and management development programme should start from the first line supervisor and go all the way up to the top management.

Selection of Techniques

The success of any Executive management development programme largely depends on the selection of the techniques. However, it should also be remembered that no single technique can prove to be sufficient, but only the combination of the techniques makes any management development programme effective. This is because all managers at all levels require all kinds of skills but in various proportions. The following table may be used in the determination of these techniques based on the needed proportions.

Teaching Techniques

Technology	*Description*	*Suitability*	*Check Point*
Lecture	All talk to explain material, with little or no participation by the class in the form of discussion and questions.	For large groups. For orientation or easy to understand material.	Unless the preparation is very good, the audience may get lost at some point and miss all of the following ideas. Short lectures and brief applications or quizzes help.
Case Study	A business problem situation is described in detail, with both relevant and irrelevant information given. The student is	For small groups. Requires discussion and participation by all participants. The case-study method is used to develop skills at	Students may get frustrated because the data are pretty much limited to the case material. Even in real life, however, similar limits are

	require to identify problems, develop alternative solutions, evaluate.	analyzing and solving complex unstructured problems and to provide broad stimulated experience. It may also be used to develop group decision-making skills.	set by time and cost. Some students fail to participate unless called upon, and others may dominate the discussion unless controlled. Arguments may evolve around opinion rather than analyzing of the "Facts" of the case
In-basket Techniques	Trainees are given a description of a company in some detail. Memos are then given to the trainees posing problems or asking for decisions.	For small groups. For developing analytical and decision-making skills. Outside data may be introduced by the trainees.	A good case and good questions are required. Considerable time may be required for discussion of students' replies.
Conference and Seminars	A speaker may lecture, or there may be no speaker, only a conference leader. Knowledge, ideas, and opinions are freely interchanged among all participants.	For broadening knowledge, stimulating new ideas, and changing attitudes. "Workshop Seminars" may be used to develop skills	Participants may stray from objects. Hardening of attitudes and conflict may occur. Seminars away from the company tend to keep politics out of the view points expressed.
Programme Instruction and Computer Assisted Learning (Learner-Control Instructor)	Programme instruction and, usually, computer assisted learning are rigid self learning devices. The student is given material and tested on it immediately before proceeding to new material.	For either large or small groups where cost is critical. Permits people to study at their own convenience.	Appropriate programmes must be available. Students may drop out by stretching out their work.
Simulation and Gaming	A business situation or an entire industry is modeled so that the student may take actions and have the results reported book back. Usually the model is stored in a computer.	For group projects. For developing decision-making skills requiring the integration of many factors.	The model should not be too simple, and the required learning of input formats should not be too complex. The student's motivation must be strong to carry out a self-development programme where reinforcement of motivation may be absent.

Remote TV like teaching	Instructor lectures to groups of students at remote class rooms. Usually, two-way voice communication is provided.	For a highly skilled lecturer working with groups of students located at widely separated company plants, this is an economical method. For courses that require relatively few questions to clarify points.	Instructors may outpace students if students do not take the initiative to slow them down. Associated written assignments have to be corrected and returned in the period between lectures to be effective.
Laboratory Training	A change agent (consultant)devices means the groups of people in an organisation to clarify their values, attitudes and problems to improve understanding, motivation, and the working climate in general	For groups of almost any size, For changing organisation's attitudes.For increasing organisational problem solving capabilities	Top management must understand its role and give strong backing to the change agent.Considerable time will be required before the impact of laboratory training becomes evident.High-level executives may have to devote a good deal of time to such programmes.
Managerial grid sessions	Six phase program lasting from three to five years. Starts with upgrading manager's skills, continues to group improvement, improves intergroup relations, goes into corporate planning, develops implementation methods, and ends with an evaluation phase.	For rapidly growing and large companies where the considerable investment has time to pay off.	Check on progress in achieving objectives.Check on turnover of the managers involved.
T-group sessions, sensitivity training, group dynamics, sessions	Participants are put in situation in which the views, behaviour and personality of each are subjected to examine and critique by the others	For developing better understanding and better perceptions of co-workers.	Participants may not be able to stand the stress involved in learning about themselves. They may withdraw from the group or suffer psychological damage. Problems arising within the group must be dissolved before the group breaks up.
Correspondence courses	Correspondence courses require students to read material on their own or	For development of technical /manual skills. For training in specialized bus-	Students must be highly motivated to study on their own. In some cases, students

	to actually work on equipment that is supplied. Students mail their answers to the company or university that offers the course. In some cases exam must be proctored by local professional teachers.	iness subjects, such as accounting. For managerial development and broadening (for e.g., the Alexander Hamilton programme).	may have friends do the home work. Proctored exams will help reduce this problem.

Suitability of various Techniques of Management/ Executive Development

Technique	***Suitability***
1. Job Rotation	This is particularly useful in the development of diversified skills and to give the executives a broader outlook, which are very important to the upper management levels.
2. Understudy	An understudy is normally chosen with forethought of making available to the organisation a subordinate who is equal to his superior in the event of retirement, illness or death of the superior. The subordinate will be able to take over his position and manage as effectively as his boss could.
3. Multiple Management	The technique is mainly useful in bringing the managers out of their narrow shells and helps them gain broader outlook knowledge in different functional areas.
4. Case Study	In the development of executives and analytical and decision making skills this technique is particularly useful.
5. Incident Method	This technique improves one's intellectual ability, practical judgment and social awareness.
6. Role Playing	Role Playing help executives in understanding people better by giving them various experiences.
7. In Basket	Situational judgment and social sensitivity are the two important qualities that can be developed with the help of this method.
8. Business Games	This technique may be used in order to develop organisational ability, quickness of thinking and leadership.
9. Sensitivity Training	This helps one know more about himself and the impact of his behaviour on the others, which are important to manage people better.
10. Stimulation	Problem solving through decision-making can be developed quite well within the help of stimulation.
11. Managerial Grid	To develop leadership qualities in executive over long period of time.
12. Conference	The most difficult thing for any one is to change his own attitude. This technique develops the ability of the executives to modify their attitudes, when needed in the interest of the organisation.

13. Lectures	This is the best technique to give more knowledge in a short period of time to a large number participant.

Career Planning

Career Planning is the process by which one selects career goals and the path of these goals. The major focus of career planning is on assisting the employees achieve a better match between personal goals and the opportunities that are realistically available in the organisation. Career programme should not concentrate only on career growth opportunities. Practically speaking, there may not be enough high level positions to make upward mobility and reality for a large number of employees. Hence, career planning efforts need to pin-point and highlight those areas that offer psychological successes instead of vertical growth.

Career Planning is not an event or end in itself, but a continuous process of developing human resources for achieving optimum results. It must, however, be noted that individual and organizational careers are not separate and distinct. A person who is not able to translate his career plan into action within the organisation may probably quit the job, if he has a choice. Organisations, therefore, should have employees in career planning so that both can satisfy each other's needs.

STAGES IN CAREER

Establishment

This is the career stage where the one begins the search for work and picks up first job. It includes the first experiences on the job, peer group evaluations, personal tensions and anxieties that confront a person trying to make his mark. This period is characterized by committing mistakes, learning from those mistakes and assuming increased responsibility. One does not reach the summit at this stage as he rarely gets a chance to handle powerful assignments. It is like going up hill, spending lot of time and energy all the while.

Mid Career

Mid career is a stage that is typically reached between the age of 35 and 50. At this point, many one may continue to show improved performance, level off or begin to decline; you are no longer viewed as a 'learner'. Mistakes committed by you would be viewed seriously and may invite penalties as well. If you are good enough, you may grow and turn out good results. If you do not have the same fire in the belly when you started your career, the best thing would be to hold on what you have. Technically speaking, a plateaued career stars at you. Plateuing is a condition of stagnating in one's current job. Since you are no longer ambitious and are more or less happy with what comes your way, the organisation can place you on job that requires experience and maturity. The organisation can't discount your worth and treat you as deadwood, since you still retain the flavor to continue to show reasonably good performance. Organisation often shows them the door or shifts them to less important jobs.

Late Career

This is the stage where one relaxes a bit and plays the part of an elder states person. For those who continued to grow through the mid-career stage, this is the time to command respect from younger employees. Your varied experiences and judgments are greatly valued and your word will carry weight; undoubtedly, you can teach others and share your experiences with others.

For those who have stagnated or deteriorated during a previous stage, the late career brings the reality that they are no longer required to run the race and its better to redirect the energies to family, friends and hobbies.

Late Stage

During this period a person's attention may turn to retirement. The achievements of a long career and the frustration and anxieties that go along with that phase are left behind. Regardless of whether one is leaving a glorified career or a dismal job, one has to make adjustments and get along with people and things

CAREER PLANNING PROCESS

Career planning is a lifelong process, which includes choosing an occupation, getting a job, growing in our job, possibly changing careers, and eventually retiring. The Career Planning offers coverage of all these areas. Career planning incorporates short-term and long-term career goals, personal goals and constraints. The task of career planning is quite a laborious one and it requires systematic planning of every step and a calculated execution. You don't always have control over outside factors such as health and family issues, but as far as possible, your planning process should incorporate the following stages:

- Short-term planning: Assess your skills, knowledge, values, constraints and interests
- Long-term planning: Identify which new skills and knowledge you want to develop.
- Research career opportunities
- Formulate a careers action plan with contingencies
- Up to 5 years ahead check the careers action plan for realism From 5 to 10 years ahead

Term Planning	Assess Your Skills, Knowledge, Values, Constraints And Interests	**Long-Term Planning**
	Identify Which New Skills And Knowledge You Want To Develop	

↓	Research Career Opportunities	↓
↓	Formulate A Careers Action Plan With Contingencies	↓
Up To 5 Years Ahead	Check The Careers Action Plan For Realism	From 5 To 10 Years Ahead

STEPS IN CAREER PLANNING PROCESS

Step One: Self Assessment: The first and foremost step in career planning is to know and assess yourself. You need to collect information about yourself while deciding about a particular career option. You must analyze your interests, abilities, aptitudes, desired lifestyle, and personal traits and then study the relationship between the career opted for and self.

Step Two: Goal Setting: Set your goals according to your academic qualification, work experience, priorities and expectations in life. Once your goal is identified, then you determine the feasible ways and objectives how to realize it.

Step Three: Academic/Career Options: Narrow your general occupational direction to a particular one by an informatory decision making process. Analyze the career option by keeping in mind your present educational qualification and what more academic degrees you need to acquire for it.

Step Four: Plan of Action: Recognize those industries and particular companies where you want to get into. Make the plan a detailed one so that you can determine for how many years you are going to work in a company in order to achieve maximum success, and then switch to another. Decide where you would like to see yourself after five years and in which position.

Step Five: Catch Hold of Opportunities: Opportunity comes but once. So, whenever you get any opportunity to prove yourself and get into your desired career, try to convert it in every way for suiting your purpose. Remember, a successful professional is also quite opportunistic in his moves, examining every opening to turn to his favor.

Advice on Career Planning

§ Try not to waste much time and wait too long between career planning sessions.

§ Don't ever judge and analyze yourself, like your likes and dislikes, abilities, etc. by listening to what people around you say. Be your best judge.

§ Be open to constructive criticisms.

§ Career planning is a very important step that needs to be considered in totality. If need be, you should not be hesitant to take the help of professional guidance and find out the best career planning for yourself

How to choose career?

Studies show that four general individual characteristics influence how people make career choices:

1. **Interests:** People tend to go after careers that they believe match their interest.
2. **Self-Image:** A career is a reflection of a person's self-image, as well as a molder of it.
3. **Personality:** this factor includes a person's personal orientation (whether one is adventurous, outgoing, passive, submissive, artistic, etc.) and personal needs (including affiliation, power and achievement needs).
4. **Social backgrounds:** Socio-economic status education and occupational status of a person's parents are covered in this category.

Career Anchors

Individuals put down anchors to stabilize their career choices. Career anchors are distinct patterns of self-perceived talents, attitudes, motivation and values that guide to stabilize a person's career after several years of real world experience and feed back. Career anchors are difficult to predict ahead of time because they are evolutionary and a result of a process of discovery. You are not very sure about them until you are confronted with a choice such as moving to head quarters or start your own business. According to Shein five forms of career anchors are:

(*a*) **Managerial Competence:** People having this drive seek managerial positions that offer opportunities for higher responsibility, decision making, power, etc.

(*b*) **Technical Competence:** People who have a strong technical or functional career anchor seem to make career choices based on the technical or functional content of the work, such as engineering, accounting.

(*c*) **Security:** If your career anchor is security, then you are willing to do what is needed to maintain job security (complying with rules, regulations of every kind) a decent income and a stable future in the form of a good retirement package.

(*d*) **Creativity:** These people are driven by an overwhelming desire to do something that is entirely of their own making. For them starting a new venture, working in a research lab, piloting a noble venture in a desert may be exciting.

(e) **Autonomy:** These people seek a career that offers freedom of action and independence.

CAREER PLANNING VS SUCCESSION PLANNING

A succession plan is a plan for identifying who is currently in post and who is available and qualified to take over in the event of retirement, voluntary retirement, dismissal or sickness. A typical succession chart shows detail of key executives and brief reference to their possible successor. The purpose of succession planning is to identify and develop people to replace current job holders in key position through succession planning, companies assure a steady flow of internal talent to fill important vacancies. Succession Planning encourages 'hiring from within' and creates a healthy environment where employees have career and not merely jobs. Succession planning helps in identifying human resource storage and skill shortages before openings occur. Thereafter it becomes easy to groom qualified candidates for further vacancies. The organisation is, thus, assured of continuity of operation and better qualified incumbents. The replacement chart is a visual representation of who will replace whom if there is a job opening. The replacement summary indicates likely replacements for each job and shows their relative strength and weakness. This can be prepared in a detailed way so as to facilitate the easy selection if a candidate in case of further vacancies.

If qualified people are not readily available within the company, outsiders can be considered for possible openings. Complete dependence on succession from within or from outside is not desirable. Internal candidates require a 'pat on the back' when they do well. External candidates are needed for injecting fresh blood into the company.

The terms career planning and succession planning are not synonymous, but they are similar. Succession planning is generally needed for key positioning at higher levels, while career planning covers executives at all levels including high skilled employees and operatives. Career planning, by its bery nature, includes succession planning. The career paths for executives are identified. How people can grow vertically is also indicated. In case of vacancy arising at any level, the career plan is well supported by a succession chart. Both are thus complimentary and interdependent.

NEED FOR CAREER PLANNING

Every employee has a desire to grow and scale new heights in his workplace. If there are enough opportunities, he can pursue his career goals and exploit his potential fully. He feels highly motivated when the organisation shows him clear path as to how he can meet his personal ambitions while trying to realize corporate goals. Unfortunately, as pointed out by John Leach, organisations do not pay adequate attention to this aspect in actual practice for a variety of reasons. The demands of employees are not matched with organisational needs, no effort is made to show how the employees can grow within certain limits, what happens to an employee five years down the line if he does well, whether the organisation is trying to offer mere jobs or long lasting careers, etc. When recognition does not come in time for meritorious performance and a certain amount of confusion prevails in the minds of employees whether they are 'in' with a chance to grow or not, they look for greener pastures outside. Key executives leave in frustration and the organisation suffers badly when turnover figures rise. Any recruitment effort made in panic to fulfill the vacancies is not going to be effective. So, the absence of career plan is going to make a big difference to both the employees and the organisation. Employees do not get right breaks at right time; there morale will be low and they are always on their toes trying to find escape routes. Organisations are not going to benefit from high employee turnover. New employees mean additional selection and training costs. Bridging the gaps through short term replacement is not going to pay in terms of productivity. Organisations, therefore, try to put their career plans in place an educate employees about the opportunities that exists internally for talented people. Without such a progressive outlook, organisations cannot prosper.

Advantages of Career Planning

A career development system tries to strike as happy balance between individual career needs and organisational workforce requirements. A number of steps are undertaken with a view to enhance career satisfaction of employees and to improve organisational effectiveness. The advantages of career planning are as follows:

1. **Benefits to employee:** The employee has advanced knowledge of career opportunities within the company. He knows where he stands, where he wants to go, who is ahead of him, how to scale the corporate ladder. This helps him set his career goals more realistically and take appropriate steps to realize them.
2. **Benefits to organisation:** Organisations can base their decisions more systematically. Fast tracks for stars could be arranged, training to slow movers can be provided, replacements can be planned in advance, hardworking, talented people can be retained through offereing attractive career options and compensation plans; job assignments can be made based on merit etc.
3. **Relations:** Relations between the employer and the employee could become more cordial; employee skills could be used properly; valued employees could be retained there will be an expanded image of the company as a people developer.

Limitations of Career Planning

1. For small units (where there are very few opportunities for the vertical growth of employees) it is not suitable.
2. Several environmental factors such as govt. policy, loss of the land, reservation based on castes, regional pressures, union demands may upset career planning and development efforts.
3. If the organisation fails to focus on any of the career related issues clearly, problems may crop up. (e.g, early career issues, mid career issues, late career issues and dual career issues etc.)

How Career Planning can Be Made Effective

To ensure the success of career planning a number of steps should be taken:

1. **Support:** Career Planning efforts must receive consistent support and continued blessings from the top management.
2. **Goals:** The corporate goals must be laid down clearly. It is not possible to develop appropriate goals for human resources, if you are not very sure about your journey in the next five or ten years.

3. **Reward Performance:** Employees must be willing to expand their abilities. Trainers must be willing to coach, counsel and share their knowledge with employees. There must be appropriate rewards for people from both sides who show promise.
4. **Placement:** Every effort must be made to put employees on jobs that are in tune with their capabilities. If a talented person is put on a routine job, he will quit in frustration.
5. **Career Paths:** the career paths for different types of employees must be laid down clearly. Fast track promotions should be available to talented people, seniors could be used on jobs requiring experience and judgment, juniors could be used for jobs that demand routine application of rules and procedures etc.
6. **Continuous Tracking:** Career Planning efforts should be carried out on a continuing basis keeping the changing needs of employees and the organisation in mind. A record of career movement of employees must be kept and periodic assessment of who has gone where should be made.
7. **Publicity:** Every one should be aware of the career opportunities within the organisation.

Case Study

Unfair Promotion

Electronic Industries Ltd, Faridabad is producing electric bulbs, water coolers, air coolers and refrigerators. Recently it had a new line of production that is electronic motors both for agricultural and domestic purposes. It needed one electric engineer with B.Tech. qualification to look after the new plant producing electric motors. Presently five electric engineers with B.E qualification as Asstt. Engineers are working in the existing plant. The company advertised for the post of chief engineer (electrical) for its new plant. It received twelve applications out of which five are Asstt. Engineers working in the existing plant. The company used techniques of preliminary interviews, tests, final interviews and medical examination and finally selected Mr. Ram Sharma, employed in the existing plant of the company. He is fourth in the seniority list of the Asstt. Engineers in the present plant. The company served the appointment letter to Mr. Ram and he joined as Chief Engineer in the new plant. But th three Asstt. Engineers in the existing plant moved the issue to the court of law contesting that the selection of Mr. Ram is not valid as he does not have seniority among the Asstt. Engineers in the existing plant.

Q.1 Is career planning important?

Summary

This chapter gives information regarding the training for special groups, executive development programmes, its evolution, techniques, characteristics, and its impediments. It also how career planning is important. The stages, process and advantages and disadvantages of career planning are emphasized.

Concept Review Questions

OBJECTIVES

1. The company also provides the first hand information to the employees about the skills needed by the company and its _________.
2. The _________trains the employee regarding various skills necessary to do the actual job.
3. ___________ training is generally used for providing technical knowledge in the areas like trades, crafts etc.
4. Executive/Management development is a systematic process of growth and development by which the _________ develop their abilities to manage.
5. The format of _________ will vary with company's size and nature of operation so as to provide optimum result.
6. _________ has an enormous impact on a firm's success.
7. _________ training takes place within the organization or outside at seminars and universities.
8. _________presents a hypothetical problem involving human interaction.

(Development programmes, trainer, apprentiship, managers, EDP, Managerial effect iveness, Classroom, role Playing)

SHORT QUESTIONS

1. What is apprenticeship training?
2. Explain executive or management development programmes.
3. What are the various techniques of MDP's
4. Write short notes on:
   (a) Lectures,
   (b) Job rotation,
   (c) Role plays,
   (d) special assignments,
   (e) Managerial grid
   (f) Johari windows
5. Explain successions planning.

6. What are the impediments to EDP's?
7. How can training be made effective?
8. What types of training are there for special groups.
9. Define the term career?
10. What do mean by career planning?
11. Write short notes on (a) career stages (b) career anchors
12. Mention two advantages of career planning
13. Differentiate between career planning and succession planning
14. How do people choose careers?
15. Mention two disadvantages of career planning

LONG QUESTIONS

1. Explain in detail management development programmes.
2. How is job rotation different from coaching.
3. Write a detailed note on succession planning.
4. Write a detailed note on the suitability of the`MDP's.
5. What is career planning? Outline the process of career planning clearly.
6. Examine the need for career planning from the point of view of an individual employee and the oragnisation
7. How career planning can be made effective?
8. What are the various steps involved in career planning?
9. Explain the need for career planning
10. What are the advantages and disadvantages of career planning?

5

Evaluation of Training

INTRODUCTION

The process of examining a training program is called training evaluation. Training evaluation checks whether training has had the desired effect. Training evaluation ensures that whether candidates are able to implement their learning in their respective workplaces, or to the regular work routines.

The specification of values forms a basis for evaluation. The basis of evaluation and the mode of collection of information necessary for evaluation should be determined at the planning stage.

The process of training evaluation has been defined as "any attempt to obtain information on the effects of training performance, and to assess the value of training in the light of that information." Evaluation leads to controlling and correcting the training programme. A vital aspect of any sort of evaluation is its effect on the person being evaluated.

Feedback is essential for people to know how they are progressing, and also, evaluation is crucial to the learner's confidence too. People can be switched off the whole idea of learning and development very quickly if they receive only negative feedback.

Purposes of Training Evaluation

The five main purposes of training evaluation are:

- **Feedback:** It helps in giving feedback to the candidates by defining the objectives and linking it to learning outcomes.
- **Research:** It helps in ascertaining the relationship between acquired knowledge, transfer of knowledge at the work place, and training.

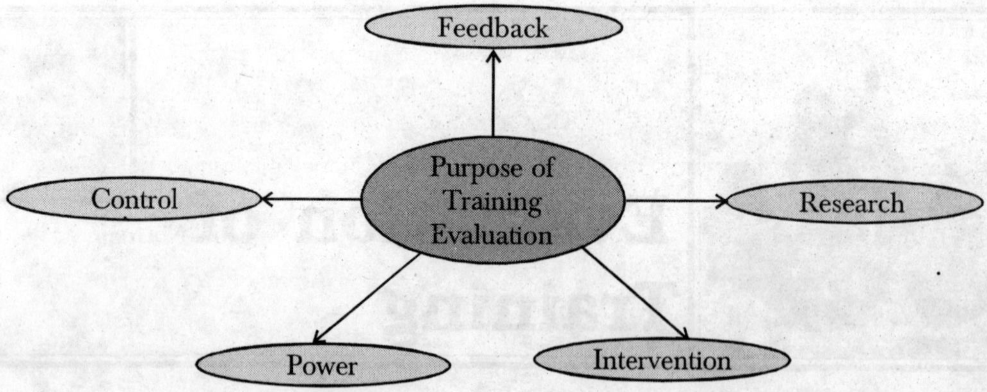

- **Control:** It helps in controlling the training program because if the training is not effective, then it can be dealt with accordingly.
- **Power games:** At times, the top management (higher authoritative employee) uses the evaluative data to manipulate it for their own benefits.
- **Intervention:** It helps in determining that whether the actual outcomes are aligned with the expected outcomes.

Types of Evaluation

The types of training are as follows:

- **Formative** evaluation provides ongoing feedback to the curriculum designers and developers to ensure that what is being created really meets the needs of the intended audience.
- **Process** evaluation provides information about what occurs during training. This includes giving and receiving verbal feedback.
- **Outcome** evaluation determines whether or not the desired results (e.g., what participants are doing) of applying new skills were achieved in the short-term.
- **Impact** evaluation determines how the results of the training affect the strategic goal e.g. health promotion goal of reducing the incidence and prevalence of HIV/AIDS.

Principles of Evaluation

Training evaluation is the process of establishing a worth of the training efforts. The term 'worth' conveys the meaning of value, merit or excellence of the input efforts. It is not merely a state of mind; rather it is a set of techniques. To achieve the desired result, evaluation has to be based on certain principles such as clarity, objectivity, reliability, evaluation design and methodology, process and not end product, and ensuring that the evaluation design is tailor made.

Clarity: The trainer or evaluator must be clear about the purpose of evaluation in order to set the standards and criteria for evaluation.

Objectivity: Demonstrating objectivity is the hall mark of a good trainer or evaluator. This requires (a) measurable standards of assessment, (b) designing of valid and reliable research instruments, and (c) analyzing and interpretation of data.

Reliability: Data must be subjected to objective analysis, for e.g., statistical analysis. Subjective analysis of data for evaluation cannot produce reliable results. For evaluation to be reliable, the result should confirm irrespective of the method you have used for data collection, if the same person collects the data again and whether interpreted by any other person. Normally, a good trainer uses more than one method of data collection and data interpretation in order to achieve reliable results.

Evaluation Design and Methodology: You have to design the methodology, considering its feasibility in regard to cost-effectiveness, practicability, and utility of the data for end-use. As such, while designing the evaluation methodology, you should ask questions like 'is it cost effective', 'is the methodology practical', and 'can the data be subjected for analysis'.

- **Cost-Effectiveness:** You should not spend more on evaluation than the estimated returns on training.
- **Practicability:** You must consider adequacy of resources, including human resource and availability of time, for executing the suggested methodology.
- **Data Usefulness:** It is possible that a lot of time and money is spent on generating evaluation data without knowing or being unable to put the same or any use whatsoever.

Process and Not End Product: Evaluation is a process and not an end product of the training system and also not the last phase of training. As such, as a process it has to be continuous. At the end of a course, you may grade the participants. Gradation is stratifying the trainees. In no ways does it help the trainer nor the training organization to improve the subsequent programmes.

Evaluation Design to be Tailor Made: Training programmes conducted by institutes on the same topic, with the same duration, and attended by participants of identical profile may widely differ in the curriculum design, methods used, use of pedagogical aids, and means of assessment. Thus, there cannot be interchangeability in the evaluation technique. It has to be tailor made to suit specific training levels and standards. Generalization drawn for one evaluation design may not identify strengths and weakness of training meant for a different set of objectives.

Thus the principles of evaluation can be concluded as:

- Evaluation specialist must be clear about the goals and purposes of evaluation.
- Evaluation must be specific.
- Evaluation must provide the means and focus for trainers to be able to appraise themselves, their practices and their products.
- Evaluation must be based on objective methods and standards.
- Realistic target dates must be set for each phase of the evaluation process. A sense of urgency must be developed, but deadlines that are unreasonably high will result in poor evaluation.

PROCESS OF TRAINING EVALUATION

The learner's skills and knowledge are assessed before the training program. During the start of training, candidates generally perceive it as a waste of resources because at most of the times candidates are unaware of the objectives and learning outcomes of the program. Once aware, they are asked to give their opinions on the methods used and whether those methods confirm to the candidates preferences and learning styles.

As such, evaluation of training incorporates the criteria of Behavioural changes that are, whether the training has caused any alteration in the behavior or not. Impact on organizational changes indicates if the modified behavior has caused positive result, such as, increased output, improved quality, and supported by cost reduction. You can group the criteria discussed as been subjective or objective. Subjective criteria rely on the participants' verbal opinions – they are asked about their impressions of the training modality and effectiveness, on the concluding day of training. Objective criteria relate to the effects of the training through measuring the specific outcomes, which can be: quantity produced, number of rejections, time taken to produce a component, etc.

The training evaluation process encompasses systematic collection of data relevant to the training need identification, selection of training methodology, adoption of training aids, value, or modification of workplace learning activities. Despite organizaions expanding a great deal of efforts and financial resources are used in setting up training and developing programs, comparatively little attention is paid to evaluation their effectiveness.

Evaluation of training is 'any attempt to obtain information (feedback) on the effects of a training programme and to assess the value of training in the light of that information for improving further training' (Hamblin 1974). Evaluation literally means the assessment of value or worth. In simple terms, it is the act of judging whether or not the activity to be evaluated is worthwhile in terms of the set criteria.

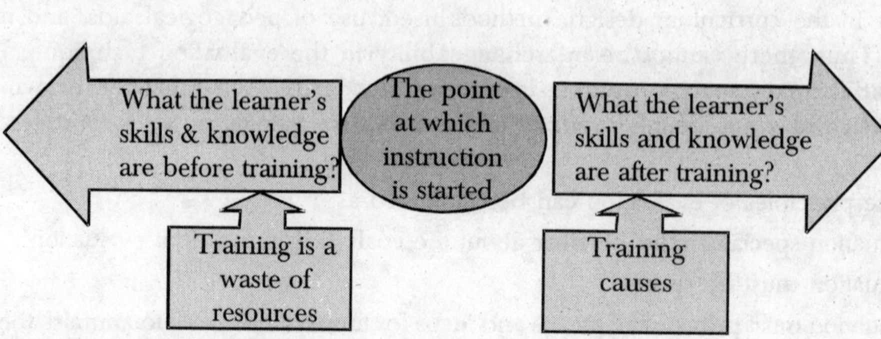

During Training: It is the phase at which instruction is started. This phase usually consist of short tests at regular intervals.

After Training: It is the phase when learner's skills and knowledge are assessed again to measure the effectiveness of the training. This phase is designed to determine whether training has had the desired effect at individual, departmental and organizational levels. There are various evaluation techniques for this phase.

Evaluation Techniques

Evaluation methods can be either **qualitative**(e.g., interviews, case studies, focus groups) or **quantitative**(e.g., surveys, experiments).

Training evaluation usually includes a combination of these methods and reframes our thinking about evaluation. The measurements are aimed at different levels of a system :

	Qualitative Methods	***Quantitative Methods***
	Exploratory Investigations	***Descriptive Surveys***
Examples	• Generating new product ideas/ concepts • Identifying key product attributes or attitudes using focus groups • Secondary data analysis (obtaining exploratory information from experts, using techniques such as Delphi, informants, archival data, case studies, journals, one-on-one interviews, etc.)	• Participant surveys to assess the differences in changes in behavior when back on the job as a result of training • Comparison of perceptions of usefulness of training • Studies to assess demographic differences between individuals/groups, etc.
Characteristics	• Is exploratory: most appropriate for exploring ideas, problem areas, concepts for design, etc. • Often used to define problem(s), identify relevant variables, and provide direction for further research	• Describes: used for description of characteristics, relationships, similarities and differences • Can suggest correlations but not prove cause/effect relationships between two or more variables (e.g., there is a correlation between attending training and changes in job related behavior, but cannot say for sure that training alone caused changes in behavior)
	• Uses fairly informal research design. • Provides depth of understanding	• Employs a well planned design that clearly identifies who, what, when, where, etc.
	• Asks "Why?"	• Asks "How many?" "How often?"
	• Is subjective • Enables discovery • Studies motivations	• Usually involves completing a questionnaire (e.g., pencil and paper instrument or telephone) to gather information
	• Allows insight into behavior, trends, etc.	• Strives to be objective
	• Interprets	• Usually involves statistical analysis

Hamblin (1974), discussed the training evaluation to illustrate the techniques used, in his study he proposes a five-level model of-reaction session, learning, job behavior, organization, and ultimate value.

- **Reaction session:** It includes reaction scales, reaction notebooks, and participation, observer's records, studies to explore inter-trainee relationships, end-of-reaction form, post-reaction questionnaires and interviews, etc.
- **Learning:** Includes tools like pre-course questionnaires to instructors, programmed instructions, objective test, typewritten or oral examinations, assessment of course content, methods used in training, presentation of faculty members, practice presentation by trainees, and so forth.
- **Job Behavior:** Includes activity sampling, observer's diaries, self-diaries with interview. Notes and questionnaires, appraisal and self-appraisal, critical incident technique, in-depth interviews, open-ended depth techniques, and prescription for involving management in the training process.
- **Organisation:** Includes indexes of productivity, labour turnover, accident rates, studies of organizational climate, use of behavioural objects, study behaviors of non-trainees, and workflow studies.
- **Ultimate Value:** Includes cost-benefits analysis and human resource accounting.

CRITERIA OF TRAINING EVALUATION

You have studied the area of application and the corresponding dimensions. It is essential to have some understanding of the criteria of evaluation. Evaluation must be planned. Otherwise, it may not fulfill the desired purpose. The criteria are:-

- **Training Validity:** Have the trainees benefited from the training programme? Did they learn during the training? If not, the validity of the training programme is not stabilized.
- **Transfer Validity:** This criterion refers to the utilization of the knowledge and skills gained through a training programme, in the work area. Thus, the question of transferring the knowledge and skill obviously arises. The ultimate question is, has the performance enhanced?
- **Intra-Organizational Validity:** Some persons may have been trained earlier and a batch may have just been trained. The performance of the recently trained batch and previously trained batch should be compared and subjected to analysis. The question is, is there consistency between the two batches?
- **Inter-Organisational Validity:** Different organizations conduct training programmes that are identical in nature. The work environment and organizational culture plays a dominant role in the effectiveness. The question here is can a training programme, validated in one organization, can be used successfully in some other organizations?

TRAINING EVALUATION MODELS

You have studied the technique of evaluation. Some points you must remember while studying or evaluating a training program are (a) observations, interviews, and questionnaire are means of gathering data and not evaluating and (b) work samples are sources of data used in evaluation .(c) Job performance is generic term for individual and group performance measures. These are measures that might help one to evaluate, provided right measures are adopted, and if you get the data you will be able to make the right analysis.

There are different approaches to evaluate training:

- Kirkpatrick's framework of four levels model.
- Jack Philips' ROI method (similar to but extended Kirkpatrick model).
- Stufflebeam' CIPP Model
- Warr et al. CIRO (context, input, reaction, outcome) Model
- Virmani and Premila Model.

Kirkpatrick's Four Levels of Training Evaluation

Donald L. Kirkpatrick first published his ideas in 1959, in a series of articles in the US training and development journals. The model has gained international acclamation and is now considered as industry standard across the HR and training communities. The model suffices the needs of industrial and commercial organizations for training and learning evaluations aimed at ongoing people development, planning, and managing training. Kirkpatrick (1998) himself redefined and updated his four levels of training evaluation model.

Kirkpatrick's Four Levels

The four levels of Kirkpatrick's evaluation model essentially measure the following:

Reaction: Evaluation at the reaction level help us to understand what the trainees think and feel about the training – their views about the training programme. This level measures the learner's perception (reaction) of the course. Learners are keenly aware of what they need to know to accomplish a task. If the training programme fails to satisfy their needs determination should be made as to whether it is the fault of the programme design or delivery. Evaluation at this level is not indicative of the trainees performance potentiality, as it does not measures what new skills the learner have acquired or what they have learned that will transfer back to the working environment. That is why, some evaluators and decision – makers downplay this value. However, the interest, attention, and motivation of the participants are critical to the success of any training programme. People learn better when they react positively to the learning environment.

Learning: Evaluation at this level attempts to answer the question, 'did the participant learn anything?' The evaluator finds what the trainees have learned from the training programme – the resulting increase in knowledge or capability. The evaluation also includes their attitudinal changes, knowledge improvement and enhanced skills. The learning evaluation requires post-training testing to ascertain the extent of learning. In addition, the post-training test is only valid when combined with the pre-training test so that you can differentiate between what they already knew prior to training and what they actually learned during the training programme. Measuring the learning that takes place in a training programme is important to validate the learning objectives. Evaluating the learning that has taken place typically focuses such questions: what knowledge was acquired, what skills were developed or enhanced, or what attitude was changed?

Behavior: Evaluation attempts to measure the effect on the job performance or the extent of behavioural modification and capability of environment, Knowledge enhancement, or application in the work performance. However, you have to keep in mind that behavior is the action that is performed, while the final results of the behavior are the performance. This evaluation involves testing the trainees' capabilities to apply the learned skills on the job, rather than in the class room. You can perform level three evaluation formally (by testing) or informally (through observing). The evaluation will help you to determine the performance is now correct by answering the questions; do people use their newly acquired knowledge on the job? Learning new skills and knowledge is no good to an organization unless the participants actually use them in their work activities.

Results: Evaluation at the preceding three levels are focused on the individuals. The fourth level of evaluation is directed towards measuring the contribution of the training efforts on the organizational performance. Evaluation at this level answers the question, what impact has the training achieved? The effects of the training programme on the business or environment resulting from the trainees performance is measured at this stage. These impacts can include such items as, efficiency, moral, team work, etc. Sometimes you may find difficulty to isolate the results of a training programme but you can definitely link training contributions to organizational improvements. Data collecting, organizing, and analyzing the data, and converting it into information can be difficult, time-consuming, and more costly than the other three levels, but the results are often worthwhile when viewed in the full context of its value to organization.

All these measures are recommended for full and meaningful evaluation of learning in organizations, although their application broadly increases in complexity, usually cost.

Jack Philips' ROI Method

The **Philips** return on investment (ROI) approach is another internationally acclaimed method to evaluate training and is endorsed by organization like The American Society of Training and Development (ASTD). This approach enables organization to calculate a financial ROI from the training event. Philip's added a fifth level to Kirkpatrick model. Dr. Philips outlines to level five in his book ***Return of Investment in Training and performance Improvement Programmes***. Some experts argue that Kirkpatrick's model does not address anything about the worth of the training. Jack Philips added a fifth level to Kirkpatrick' Approach, and called it ROI or return on investment to get an answer to the question, did the training pay for itself? Can the effort, time spent, and expenditure incurred for the training is justified? If it can, then the expenditure will be treated as investment to enhance the potential of human assets. Philips' introduced the fifth level for the first time considering the need for the evaluator to appreciate the finer workings of the organization and also employ some skills in determining cost and benefit.

RETURN ON INVESTMENT

ROI is an accounting valuation method and the traditional financial measure based on historic data. Organisations are investing in training and development, and computing the result on the investment. As such, ROI is a backward-looking metric. In the field of academics, the return on investment has been used primarily for self-justification rather than continuous improvement.

To calculate monetary ROI, identify the total financial benefit to your organization (can be derived from a learning programme) and then subtract it from the total investment made to develop, produce, and execute the programme. It is truly difficult to measure all the cost associated with the programme and even harder to isolate the financial benefits from the programme. But you will find this exercise worth completing once in a while so that you can assess the types of statistics you are tracking to and if they are right once to measure. More regularly, you should also examine what creates non-financial value, such as motivation, behavioural modification, dealing with peers, time spent at the work place, absenteeism, accident rate, etc.

The ROI is measured as total benefit less total cost as a percentage of total cost

$$\frac{\text{Total Benefit} - \text{Total Cost}}{\text{Total Cost}} \times 100 = ROI$$

Total benefits include money saved by the organization, money made, and anything that adds directly or indirectly to the bottom line.

The elements of total cost broadly include the obvious and the not-so-obvious costs, namely, development cost, trainees type away from the workplace, expenditure in performing a journey (if applicable), overhead of education department, physical material, needs/refreshment facilities, cost of coordination, cost of job, coverage during training, programme materials, overhead instructions, depreciation of building, utilities and facilities, etc. In the case of online courses the elements further include servers, graphics, web development, and maintenance. Of course, some elements decrease also.

CIPP Approach to Evaluation

Daniel Stufflebeam develops the CIPP model of training evaluation in the 1960s. CIPP is an acronym for context, input, process and product. Obviously, this model requires the evaluation of context, input, process, and product in judging the value of a programme. Stufflebeam developed this model as a means of linking evaluation with programme decision making. Planning, structuring, implementing, and reviewing and revising decision from a training cycle. CIPP framework provides an analytical and rational basis for programme decision making, and conforming the cycle.

CIPP is a decision – focused approach to evaluation. This approach emphasizes the systematic provision of information for programme management and operation. An information resource is viewed as the most valuable in this approach, as information helps programme managers to make better decisions. As such, evaluation activities should be planned to fulfill the decision needs of the programme staff. Obviously, a programme can always change during execution. Accordingly, evaluation activities have to adapt to meet these changing needs as well as ensuring continuity of focus.

Thus CIPP framework aims to link evaluation with programme decision making. The model further provides an analytical and rational basis for programme decision making, based on a cycle of planning, structuring, implementing, and reviewing and revising decisions, each exclaimed through a different aspect of evaluation – context, input, process, and end product evaluation.

Stufflebeam viewed evaluation in terms of the type of decisions it served and categorized it according to its functional role within a system of planned change. The CIPP model is an attempt to make evaluation directly relevant to the needs of decision-makers during the different phases and activities of a programme. One of the problems with this evaluation in general is getting its findings used. CIPP aims to ensure that the decision-makers in a project use its findings as its primary concern is helping the decision-making process. CIPP also takes a holistic approach to evaluation, and aims to highlight a broad picture of understanding of a programme and its context and the processes at work.

CIPP emphasizes the systematic provision of information for programme management and operation. It is a decision-focused approach to evaluation. Information is seen as most valuable and helping the managers of learning (programme director, programme coordinator) to make better decisions. The evaluation activities are planned to coordinate with the decision needs of programme managers. Thereafter evaluators undertake data collection and reporting to promote more effective programme management. The programme may change during execution. In such cases, decision-makers change the evaluation activities to adopt and adjust with the changing needs, as well as to ensure continuity of focus wherever appropriate. Changing the evaluation criteria is required in order to trace development and performance over time.

In the CIPP approach, in order to be useful, the evaluation must address the questions in ways and language that they will easily understand and interpret. The approach attempts to involve the decision-makers in the evaluation planning process as a way of increasing the likelihood of the evaluation findings having relevance and being used. Stufflebeam thought it imperative that evaluation should be a process of delineating, obtaining, and providing useful information to decision-makers, with the overall goal of programme or project improvement.

Stufflebeam views purpose of evaluation as:

- Establishing and providing useful information for judging decision alternatives
- Assisting an audience to judge and improve the worth of some educational programme or subject
- Assisting the improvement of policies and programmes

The four aspects of CIPP evaluation (context, input, process and product) help the decision-maker to get answer to four basic questions:

What should we do? To get an answer to this you have to collect and analyze needs assessment data to determine goals, priorities, and objectives. For e.g., context evaluation of a programme on 'training of trainers' might involve an analysis of the existing objectives of the programme, developing trainers' skill as can be evidenced in the practice lecture sessions, and perceptions, or attitudes and needs.

How should we do it? This involves the steps and resources needed to impart the skills to train young and elderly persons, and might include identifying the strength, weaknesses, and personal convictions of participants.

Are we doing it as planned? If you comply with the plan, it would be possible to provide information to the decision-makers about how well the programme is being implemented. You are required to continuously monitor the programme. Decision-makers will be able to know things such as how well the programme is following the plans and guidelines, staff support and moral, strengths and weaknesses of reading material.

Did the programme work? You must measure or observe the outcomes and compare them to anticipated outcomes to understand the gap. This will enable decision-makers to decide whether the programme should be continued, modified, or dropped altogether. This is the essence of product evaluation.

CIRO Approach

Warr et al. (1970) propounded the CIRO (context, input, reaction, and outcome) model. Almost four decades have elapsed but the CIRO model still remains one of the most widely used training evaluation models. The model strikes a chord with some of the key issues that trainers are still grappling with today-how to demonstrate the impacts of training on organizational objectives, and in turn, how to make a strong business case for training.

In the CIRO evaluation approach there are four components (context, input, reaction, and outcome) of evaluation and the evaluation can occur at two levels – at the organizational level and at a single-event level such as training programme. At the organizational level, the purpose of evaluation is to measure the success of the employee's development strategy. This specifically assesses whether the planned objectives have been achieved. Employee development strategies depend on the size and the industry to which it belongs. The basic purpose of training including induction programmes may be different; the aim of a large-scale industry may be to look at a wealth of schemes while that of a small-scale company may be its mere survival. Any programme that requires huge resources like management time and cost should be regularly evaluated.

At the single-event level, the purpose of evaluation is to asses how that particular event fits into the overall training cycle (business needs, identifying training needs, specifying training needs, translating training needs into actions, planning the training, and finally evaluating the training), which is a series of sequential steps that businesses need to go through in order to deliver effective training and development.

If you adopt the CIRO approach to evaluate training, you will get the opportunity to follow a model while conducting training and development assessment. A key benefit using the CIRO approach is that it ensures that all aspects of a training cycle are covered. You should conduct training evaluation in following areas:

Context: Context refers to the environment within which the training took place. Training management must objectively identify training needs through man, task, and organizational analysis. Evaluation here is directed to pinpointing the reasons for the training or development event, and the system or strategy of need identification. The training manager should look at the methods used to decide on the original training or development specification. Unless this is done, the training might not produce results. You need to look at how the information was analyzed and how the needs were identified.

Inputs: Evaluation of the planning and design processes – which leads to the selection of trainers, programmes, pedagogy, employees, and materials – involves re-thinking and determining the appropriateness and accuracy of the inputs, which is crucial to the success of the training or development initiative. If for e.g., someone without any flair and aptitude for teaching attends a programme on training of trainers, they are likely to cause hindrance to the learning process. Not only will they not learn, but they are likely to jeopardize the environment, ultimately leading to waste of time and money for the organization.

• **Reactions** – The method of evaluation at the reaction stage should be appropriate to the nature of the training undertaken. Management may want to measure the reaction of learners to the training and assess the relevance of the training course to the roles performed by the learners. The assessment is directed to the content and presentation of the training event to evaluate its quality.

Outcomes: Management may want to measure the extent of learning transferred to the workplace. This is easier where the training is concerned with the hard and specific skills; for e.g., if a machine operator is trained on machine technology, selecting speed, feed, and depth of cut, relating to the material to be machined, one can measure the out come of the training programme from the average number of components produced over a period. Thus, the records of pre-training and post-training performance levels of the learners are the relevant objective evidences. The average production before and after will directly indicate the outcome. But, softer and less quantifiable competencies including behavioural skills cannot always be measured.

In addition to evaluating the context, input, reactions, and outcomes to training and development management must continuously measure the associated cost. You can carry out a cost-benefit analysis prior to committing into any training initiative. Costs must be monitored to ensure that they do not scale over budget.

Evaluation Methods: There are several evaluation methods that can be used. These range from learner's feedback through discussions, surveys, and questionnaires to more rigorous testing methods. The method must be appropriate to the learning objective. Timing is important. The greater the time delay between the training event and evaluation, the less reliable the results are likely to be, since there will be factors other than the training that may well have had an effect on the outcome.

Virmani and Premila Model

Jiwani (2006) had taken up a study to find out the most effective training methods that help in ensuring learning and its transfer real-life situations, based on **Virmani and Premila's** model of training evaluation. He based the training design of the programme on the research done by World Health Organization (WHO) on skill sets required to succeed in a competitive society. The broad objective of the programme was to equip the students with the skills required to deal effectively with the demands and challenges of the global environment. Jiwani (2006) mentions the three stages proposed by Virmani and Premila.

The stages are follows:

Stage I: Pre-training evaluation: At this stage he sent pre-training questionnaires to the trainees 15 days prior to the programme. Then he discussed components of the programme at the pre-programme meet. The objectives of the pre-training evaluation were (a) to ascertain the expectations of the trainees and (b) to ensure goal congruence of the objectives between the trainers and the trainees.

Stage II: Context and input evaluation: At this stage he used to collect the data of the pre-training evaluation questionnaires and documents of the pre-programme meet. He attempted to understand the background of each participant and to get a direction of the pedagogogical tools relevant to achieve the set objectives.

Stage III: Post-training evaluation: he embarked on the reaction evaluation and learning evaluation processes. The objectives were to capture the immediate feelings of the trainees with reference to certain parameters.

VALIDATION OF TRAINING PROGRAMME

Validation of training programme means justification, rationality and providing supportive information of conducting the training and directly refers and applies to the programme and its immediate results. Validation is categorized and defined as internal validation and external validation. Validation deals with a series of tests and assessment designed to ascertain both the categories of validation.

Internal Validation

In internal validation, the focus is on the closeness and nearness of the training and learning, resulting in improvements, gaining knowledge and enhancing the skills of the trainee. These, in turn, contribute to the enhancement of organizational performance.

External Validation

An organization has to objectively identify the training needs and provide the training to achieve the business goals. External validity involves a series of analysis designed to ascertain whether the objectives of an internally valid programme are based on accurate information in relation to the criteria of training needs. This is to ensure that:

(*a*) Training is carried out in the most efficient and effective manner.

(*b*) Training is at the lowest or most reasonable cost, without compromising on the quality of training.

(*c*) The training has a high implementation value.

Impediments to Effective Training

There are many impediments which can make a training programme ineffective. Following are the major hindrances:

1. **Management Commitment is Lacking and Uneven:** Most companies do not spend money on training. Those that do, tend to concentrate on managers, technicians and professionals. The rank-and-file workers are ignored. This must change, for, as a result of rapid technological change, combined with new approaches to organizational design and production management, workers are required to learn three types of new skills:
   (*i*) The ability to use technology
   (*ii*) The ability to maintain it
   (*iii*) The ability to diagnose system problems

In an increasingly competitive environment, the ability to implement rapid changes in products and technologies is often essential for economic viability.

2. **Aggregate Spending on Training is Inadequate:** Companies spend minuscule proportions of their revenues on training. Worse still, budget allocations to training are the first item to be cut when a company faces a financial crunch.
3. **Educational Institutes Award Degrees but Graduates Lack Skills:** This is the reason why business must spend vast sums of money to train workers in basic skills. Organisations also need to train employees in multiple skills. Managers, particularly at the middle level, need to be retrained in team-playing skills, entrepreneurship skills, leadership and customer-orientation skills.
4. **Large-Scale Poaching of Trained Workers:** Trained work force is in great demand. Unlike Germany, where local business groups pressure companies not to poach on another company's employees, there is no such system in our country. Companies in our country, however, insist on employees to sign 'bonds of tenure' before sending them for training, particularly before deputing them to undergo training in foreign countries. Such bonds are not effective as the employees or the poachers are prepared to pay the stipulated amount as compensation where the bonds are breached.
5. **No Help to Workers Displaced Because of Downsizing:** Organisations are downsizing and delayering in order to trim their work forces. The government should set apart certain fund from the *National Renewable Fund* for the purpose of retraining and rehabilitating displaced workers.
6. **Employers and B Schools Must Develop Closer Ties:** B schools are often seen as not responding to labour-market demands. Business is seen as not communicating its

demands to B Schools. This must change. Businessmen must sit with Deans and structure the courses that would serve the purpose of better business.

7. **Organized Labour can help:** Organized labor can play a positive role in imparting training to workers. Major trade unions in our country seem to be busy in attending to mundane issues such as bonus, wage, revision, settlement of disputes and the like. They have little time in imparting training to their members.

IMPROVING EFFECTIVENESS OF TRAINING

The training programmes can be made effective and successful if the following hints are considered:

1. Specific training objectives should be outlined on the basis of the type of performance required to achieve organizational goals and objectives. An audit of personal needs compared with operational requirements will help to determine the specific training needs of the individual employees. This evaluation should form a well-defined set of performance standards towards which each trainee should be directed.
2. Attempt should be made to determine if the trainee has the intelligence, maturity, and motivation to successfully complete the training programmes. If deficiencies are noted in these respects, the training may be postponed or cancelled till improvements are visible.
3. The trainee should be helped to see the need for training by making him aware of the personal benefits he can achieve through better performance. He should be helped to discover the rewards and satisfaction that might be available to him through changes in behaviour.
4. The training programme should be planned so that it is related to the trainee's previous experiences and background. This background should be used as a foundation for development and new behaviour.
5. Attempts should be made to create organizational conditions that are conducive to a good learning environment. It should be made clear why changes are needed. Any distractions, in the way of training environment, should be removed. The support of the upper levels of management should be obtained before applying training at lower levels.
6. If necessary, a combination of training methods should be selected so that variety is permitted and as many of the senses as possible are utilized.
7. It should be recognized that all the trainees do not progress at the same rate. Therefore, flexibility should be allowed in judging the rates of progress in the training programme.
8. If possible, the personal involvement or the active participation of the trainee should be got in the training programme. He should be provided with opportunities to practice the newly needed behavioural norms.
9. As the trainee acquires new knowledge, skills and attitudes and applies them in job situations, he should be significantly rewarded for his efforts.
10. The trainee should be provided with regular, constructive feedback concerning his progress in training and implementation of the newly acquired abilities.

11. The trainee should be provided with the personal assistance when he encounters learning obstacles.

TRAINING AND ORGANISATION

Failure of training is not always because of lack of KSAs but sometimes it is because of the organizational forces also. These forces also hold back the transfer of training, and learning. Therefore, it is important to keep in check those forces. For the successful transfer of training, it is necessary to have supervisor support, trainer support, peer support, reward system, climate and culture.

- **Peers Support**: Peer support can also help in transfer of training, for example, if the trainee is the only one who is receiving training in the department then probably the experienced peers might put pressure on trainee to forget the training and work. This situation also hampers in transfer of training. However, this situation can be avoided by involving the entire department in training, also by encouraging the learning culture in the organization.

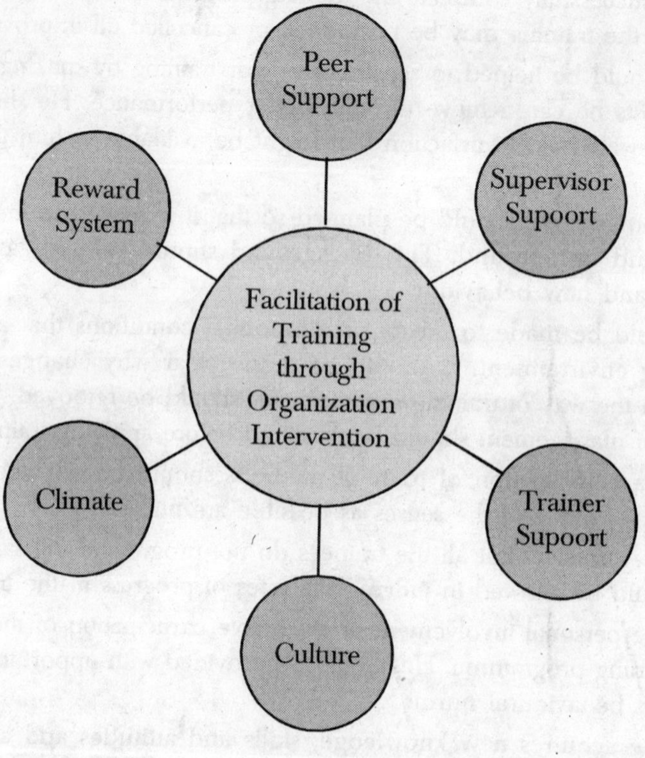

- **Supervisor Support**: can affect their employees learning in number of ways, for example, if the trainee is motivated to learn and receives full support from his supervisor, then this support in turn encourages the employee to learn as much as possible. Also, supervisor can also reduce the negative factors of training, such as, the work that piles up during training that makes the employee uncomfortable and employees' negative perception about the training program.

- **Trainers' Support**: can also have a positive impact on the transfer of training. Gone are the days, when the trainers' role used to get over once the training program is done. Trainers' role is now extended to the work place also. Besides training, trainer's role is to keep a check on how trainees are performing and help them and discuss with them if they encounter any problem in the workplace.
- **Climate**: Apart from supervisor support, peers support, trainer support, Climate factor also comprises of company polices, attitude of upper management towards employees and towards training. If these factors are positive then the climate will also support the transfer of training. It is the organizations foremost duty to make the employees realize that through these factors adequate amount of time and resources are spent on them for their professional and personal development.
- **Culture**: also have the impact over the transfer of training. If the culture of the organization provides enough opportunities to its employees to implement what they have learnt in the workplace and provide them variety of others factors such as, social support, challenging jobs, etc then the likelihood of the transfer of training increases.
- **Reward Systems**: If the learning outcome that helps in achieving the objectives is linked to reward system then the probability of the success of training would increase.

To put training program into effect according to definite plan or procedure is called training implementation. Training implementation is the hardest part of the system because one wrong step can lead to the failure of whole training program. Even the best training program will fail due to one wrong action.

Case Study

TRAINING EVALUATION LEADS TO EFFECTIVENESS

Ultratech Mechanical Works (UMW) is located in an industrial area. It has three cost centers.

Hydraulic division, Automobile division, and Textile machinery division. UMW produces components, sub-assemblies, and assemblies. It has a tool room that produces tools and gauges for all cost centers. The company has a mechanical and an electrical maintenance department, offices, store, quality control section, and a training department. The manpower strength of the company is 2,100. The company has contracts with Control Tool Room (CTR) and Training Centre (CTTC), Bhubneshwar, and Advanced Training Institute (ATI), Kolkata, for training the company personal. In 2004, it started its own training department to conduct in-house training programme.

The company received a bulk order for engine pistons a year ago. As per the contractual agreement, the pilot batch of 20 components was developed and submitted to the client, who gave the green signal to start bulk manufacturing. The contract also specifies the schedule of delivery –

2000within six months after approval of bulk and 750 every month in the first year, thereafter. The component (engine piston) needs certain special skills in regards to positional accuracy and on certain zones, the component needs induction hardening.

Considering the quality and quantity to be manufactured, the company assigned the task to three experienced turners, and in turn, engaged three semi-skilled machinists to their job. However the company decided to develop some craftsmen through training in the company's training department. Accordingly four turners and six machinists were selected from all the three cost centers for two week training and therefore relieved from doing their regular tasks. The topics included blueprint reading, interpretation of position symbols, speed and feed, depth of cut, preservation of semi-finished components, heat treatment technology, and hands-on sessions. The person in-charge of training designed the syllabus and the production manager approved it. The ten employees of the company attended the theoretical classes and practical demonstrations. On the concluding day, as a ritual, feed backs were taken from the participants. Most of the participants expressed their utmost satisfaction with the course. On completing the training, they were assigned tasks in the operations of engine pistons as well as their regular jobs. Now, UMW started maintaining records of production. The average production of the trained operators was lower than the average production of the experienced operators. Added to this, the quality was also inferior as evidence from the rejection. The woks manager called on the production manager to enquire into the matter and requested him to be more vigilant. The CEO of the company (A.K Jawahar) Learnt about the shortcomings of the trained persons. He ordered a senior manager (Mr. SP) to investigate the matter. Mr. SP was earlier the training manager in another company and had established the training department of UMW also.

He meticulously investigated and submitted his report. The salient features of the report are produced:

(*a*) Competencies required to manufacture the engine piston were not identified while preparing the course content.

(*b*) Training need was not identified based on a man, task, and organizational analysis.

(*c*) Attributes necessary for production were not identified and hence ignored.

(*d*) Profiles of participants were heterogeneous.

(*e*) Many faculty members did not know the purpose of the training.

(*f*) The training department

- Did not make any programme of the training
- Did not maintain any record of lectures
- Intimated the trainer just a day before
- Did not produce the full programme for the trainers

Mr. Jawahar convened a meeting, requesting the presence of the planning manager, training manager, person in-charge of training, and the senior manager Mr. SP. At the meeting, in the presence of all, Mr. Jawahar directed them to collect all relevant data, pursue an in-depth analysis and decide a future course of action. Unfortunately, data could not be retrieved, as they were not maintained. Finally, the purpose of the training was defined, training specification was prepared, programme was planned, all training-related information was issued to faculty members and demonstrators, with a copy of the blueprint of the engine piston, and a seven-day training programme was held. UMW observed distinct behavioural modification, attitudinal change, and rise in production confirming to qualitative requirements.

Q Does training leads to effectiveness?

Summary

This chapter gives a detailed knowledge about the evaluation of training. It is necessary to evaluate the extent to which the training programs have achieved the aims for which they were designed. Purpose of training evaluation along with its types and principles are also given in this chapter. It also gives a detailed information regarding the process of training evaluation, techniques of training evaluation , criteria of training evaluation and the models of training evaluation.It also throws light on the validation of training programmes along with the impediments to effective training and how training can be made effective. The relationship between of training and organization and its various components are also specified.

Concept Review Questions

OBJECTIVES

1. The process of examining a training program is called _________.
2. Evaluation leads to _________ & _________the training programme.
3. Training evaluation is the _________ of establishing a worth of the training efforts.
4. _________is generic term for individual and group performance measures.
5. _________ is an accounting valuation method and the traditional financial measure based on historic data.
6. Daniel Stufflebeam develops the _________model of training evaluation in the 1960s.
7. Most companies do not spend money on ________.
8. Failure of training is not always because of lack of _________ but sometimes it is because of the organizational forces

(training evaluation, controlling/correcting, process, Job Performance, ROI, CIPP, training, KSAs)

SHORT QUESTIONS

1. What do you mean by evaluation of training?
2. What are the purposes of the training evaluation?
3. What are the various types of evaluation of training?
4. How are reward systems and supervisor support helpful in facilitating training in the organization?
5. Differentiate between internal and external validation?
6. What is CIPP Approach to Evaluation?
7. What are Kirkpatrick's Four Levels of Training Evaluation?
8. What is Jack Philips' ROI Method of evaluation?
9. Explain the Virmani and Premila Model of training evaluation?
10. What is the difference between Inter Organizational Validity and Intra Organizational Validity?

LONG QUESTIONS

1. Explain the various steps and methods of training evaluation.
2. What are the factors that are helpful in facilitating training in the organization?
3. Why do organizations often overlook or lack proper evaluation of training programs.
4. What are the impediments to training?
5. How can training be made effective?
6. Explain in detail the various models of training?

PREVIOUS YEAR QUESTION PAPERS

BBA Examination 2009

SECTION–A

Q1. "How can we develop a training programme which will have a significant impact on the new first line supervisors, experienced supervisors (first and second level) and on staff personnel, both new and experienced?

This was the question we faced at Doon Bearings a company at SIDCUL, Haridwar............at an initial task force meeting of seven middle managers. The challenge had been issued to the task force by the two vice-presidents of major divisions (manufacturingand distribution) to build a practical, participative, results oriented training programme for newly appointed unit managers, the company's title for first-line supervisors.

Questions:

(*i*) Describe the steps you would go through before actually designing the content of the training.

(*ii*) How would you evaluate the training modules to determine how effective it was?

(*iii*) Do you think these line managers were the right people to design the training programme? Who else would you add, if anyone, to this group?

SECTION – B

Q2. Write short notes on any four of the following:

(*i*) Benefits of training to employees

(*ii*) Induction or Orientation Training

(*iii*) Vestibule Training

(*iv*) Training Objectives

(*v*) Job Rotation

(*vi*) Reinforcement of Learning

(*vii*) Career Planning

(*viii*) Career Path

Q3. Discuss the various types of training programmes prevalent in the industry?

Or

Explain the various principles of learning which are relevant for imparting training to workers.

Q4. Why is needs assessment an important first step in any training programme? Explain how the training needs of employees can be identified?

Or

Explain the essential steps of a good training programme.

Q5. What do you understand by career planning? Describe its need and objectives.

Or

Write short notes on the following:

(*a*) Executive Development Programmes

(*b*) Systems Approach to Training

BBA EXAMINATION 2008

SECTION – A

Q1. What is the significance of training for employees in the organization? What are the different methods of training? Discuss with suitable expamles.

SECTION – B

Q2. Write short notes on any four of the following:

(*i*) Vestibule Training

(*ii*) Role of trainers

(*iii*) Principle of learning

(*iv*) Job Analysis

(*v*) Motivation and training

(*vi*) Importance of Training evaluation

(*vii*) Training assessment

Q3. Discuss the process of training in an organization. How the training needs are determined?

Or

What is the psychology of learning? How does the learning principle help in training and development of the employees?

Q4. What are the factors considered for developing a training programme? What are the limitations of on the job training?

Or

Discuss the various contents of Executive Development Programme for a service organization.

Q5. How the training effectiveness is evaluated? How is the feedback of participants evaluated effectively?

Or

How does training significantly enhance the career planning of employees? How training is relevant for the productivity of the organization?

BBA EXAMINATION 2007

SECTION – A

Q1. The Punjab Bank Ltd., had been facing problems relating to deposit mobilization and loan recovery. The bank appointed a number of commissions to go into the problems and find out the root cause for these problems. All the commissions pointed out that the delay in decision making and faulty decisions made by the executives at different levels are responsible for the state of affairs in the bank. Mr. Pande, the Chairman of the Bank asked the chief personnel manager to develop various techniques and organize executive development programs in order to improve the decision making skills of the Bank executives from the level of the branch manager to the general manager.

The Chairman himself attended and executive development program conducted by the Administrative Staff College of India for Chairmen of the all the Bank. He was very impressed by two techniques in the entire program. They were role playing and sensitivity training and strongly felt that these techniques should be used in the proposed executive development program at the Bank. He called the Chief Personnel Manager of the Bank and told him about his experience and ideas. But the Chief Personnel Manager responded negatively. Mr. Pande tried his best to convince the Chief Personnel Manager and similarly the Chief Personnel Manager also tried to persuade Mr. Pande about the nature of those techniques and the nature of the proposed development program. At last Mr. Pande vexed with the behavior of the Chief Personnel Manager ordered him to use role playing and sensitivity training techniques.

Questions:

(*i*) Do you find any justification in the argument of Mr. Pande?

(*ii*) Why did Mr. Pande form such an opinion?

(*iii*) What do you feel about the suitability of technique for the executive development programme in this case?

SECTION – B

Q2. Write short-notes on any four of the following(up to 50 words):

(*a*) What is the difference between training and development?

(*b*) What is learning?

(*c*) Which factors can motivate a person to learn?

(*d*) What qualities should trainers have to make training effective?

(*e*) What is job rotation?

(*f*) What is the purpose of establishing training objectives in any training programme?

(*g*) What are learning principles?

(*h*) Why is it important to evaluate training?

Q3. What are the important steps in the development of a training programme? Describe the steps in detail?

Or

Explain the various principles of learning which are relevant for imparting training to workers.

Q4. Distinguish between Training and Management Development?

Or

What do you understand by career planning? Describe its need and objectives.

Q5. How will you determine the training needs of an industrial organization? Discuss.

Or

How are training programmes evaluated?

Bibliography and Web References

§ Aswathappa, K. (2006), Human Resource and Personnel Management, Tata McGraw Hill 5th addition.

§ K. Ashwathapa, Human Resource Management. Tata McGraw Hill 5th addition.

§ Berliner, W. And M. C. Larney, Management Practice and Taining, Homewood, 1974.

§ Charis Hendry, Human Resource Management, B. H. Contemporary Business Series, 1995.

§ Bee, Frances and Roland, Bee (2000), Training needs analysis and evaluation, University Press (India) Ltd., Hyderabad.

§ Craig Robert L., and Lester R. Brittle (ED), Training and Development Handbook, McGraw Hill.

§ Craig Robert L., and Bittie Lester, Taining and Development Handbook.

§ Development, Deep and Deep Publications Pvt. Ltd. New Delhi.

§ Dayal, Ishwar, Management Training in Organisation, Prentice Hall of India, New Delhi, 1970.

§ Dessler Gray, Human Resource Management, Prentice Hall of India, New Delhi, 2000.

§ Givin, Robert M., Personnel Taining, McGraw Hill, New York, 1965.

§ Hacon, R. J., Management Training, Aims and Methods, English University Press.

§ Lynton, Rolf P. and Udai Pareek (2000), Training and Development (22nd Addition), Vistaar Publication (A division of sage publication)new Delhi.

§ Mager, Robert F.(1999), HRD Training and Development, Volume – 2, JAICO Publishing House, Delhi.

§ Nakkiran, S. and M. Karthikeyan (2007), Training Techniques for management.

§ Newstrom, J. W.and M.L.Lengnick(1991), 'One size does not fit all', Training and Development Journal, 45(6), American society For Training and Development.

§ Philip Darling, Training for Profits, McGraw Hill.

§ Reddy, Dr. Rathan B. 2005, Effective Human Resource Training and Development strategy, Himalya Publishing House, Delhi.

§ Srivastava, V.N., M. Shafiq and K. Ghosh (2005), 'Higher Performance Management through systematic efforts', Indian Journal of Training and Development, October – December 2005.

§ Taylor, V. B. and G. Lippit, Management Development and Training Handbook, McGraw Hill, New York.

§ Usher, R. ,I. Bryant and R. Johnston (1997), Adult Education and the Post-Modern Challenge: Learning Beyond the limits, Routledge, London, pp.94 (www.are.edu. au)

§ Virmani, B. R. and Premila Seth, Evaluating Management Training and Development, Vision Books.

§ Werner, John M.,L.Randy and L.DeSimone(2007), Human Resource Development, 4e, Thomson South-Western, Thomson Learning, Delhi.

§ Wilson, John P.(2005),Human Resource Development-Learning and Training for Individuals and Organizations ,Kogan Page Ltd.,New Delhi.

WEB RESOURCES

§ www.hrmguide.net – Human Resource Management

§ www.hrtopics.com – Human Resource News and Releases

§ www.hrmguide.com - HRM Related Articles, Features and Links

§ www.www.ollie.dccd.edu - Assessment of Job Performance

§ www.thomsonlearning.co.uk/businessandmanagement/corenelinus/links.htm

§ www.ecu.edu.au/library/faculty/fac - HR Information

§ www.humanresources.about.com

§ www.questia.com/library - Job Evaluation - Appraising Employee Performance

Glossary

A

Action Learning: is the approach that links the world of learning with the world of action through a reflective process within small cooperative learning groups known as 'action learning sets'.

Andragogy: refers to adult learning.

Apprenticeship training: refers to training on basic skills and knowledge in specified trades to educated employees/apprentices with a view to improving their employment opportunities or to enable them to start their own industry.

Audio visuals: include television, slides, overheads, videotapes and films.

C

Case study: is a written description of an actual situation in business which provokes, in the reader, the need to decide what is going on, what the situation really is or what the problems are, and what can and should be done.

Career planning: is a lifelong process, which includes choosing an occupation, getting a job, growing in our job, possibly changing careers, and eventually retiring.

Career anchors: are distinct patterns of self: perceived talents, attitudes, motivate and values that guide to stabilize a person's career after several years of real world experience and feed back

Conference: Discussion on decision making on training needs identification.

Counseling: It refers to discussion between a training practitioner and the person seeking guidance

Coaching: refers to the process where employees are coached and instructed by skilled co: workers, by supervisors, by the special training instructors.

Committee assignments: refers to the process where a group of trainees are given and asked to solve an actual organizational problem.

D

Development: refers to those learning opportunities designed to help employees grow.

E

Education: refers to Learning or acquiring orderly, logical systems for processing new information.

F

Formative Evaluation: provides ongoing feedback to the curriculum designers and developers to ensure that what is being created really meets the needs of the intended audience.

I

Impact Evaluation: determines how the results of the training affect the strategic goal.

J

Job instruction training (jit): refers to training through step by step learning.

Job rotation: refers to moving employees from job to job to add variety and reduce boredom by allowing them to perform a variety of tasks.

L

Learning: is the process of encoding, retaining, and using information.

Learning principles: are guidelines to the ways in which people learn most effectively.

Lecture: is a verbal presentation of information by an instructor to a large audience.

M

Manager: is any person who supervises others.

Management development: is a systematic process of growth and development by which the managers develop their abilities to manage.

Mission: tells about the identity that how the organization would like to be viewed by the customers, employees, and all other stakeholders.

Manpower analysis: refers to analysis of the persons to be trained and the changes required in the knowledge, skills and aptitudes of an employee are determined.

O

On the job training: Under this method, the individual is placed on a regular the job and taught the skills necessary to perform that job.

Off: the job training: Under this method of training, trainee is separated from the job situation and his attention is focused upon learning the material related to his future job performance

Organizational Climate Analysis: refers to the prevailing climate of an organization that reflects the member's attitudes

P

Process Evaluation: provides information about what occurs during training. This includes giving and receiving verbal feedback.

Programmed instruction: is a method where training is offered without the intervention of a trainer.

R

Reinforcement: refers to something positive to be reinforced to memory and to the system, again and again, until it becomes a spontaneous affair.

Resource Utilization Analysis: refers to the allocation of human and physical resources and their efficient utilization in meeting the operational targets

Role playing: is a method of human interaction which involves realistic behavior in the imaginary situations.

Role of Organization: The role of the company in management development is to establish the programme and the development opportu: nities for its present and potential managers

S

Simulation: is a technique that duplicates as nearly as possible the actual conditions encountered on the job.

Sensitivity training: is a group training method that uses intensive participation and gives immediate feedback for self analysis and change.

Seminar: this method involves a group of people who pose ideas, examine and share facts, ideas and data, test assumptions and draw conclusions, of which contribute to the improvement of job performance.

System: is a combination of things or parts that must work together to perform a particular function.

T

Training: is a short term educational process and utilizing a systematic and organized procedure by which employees learn technical knowledge and skills for a definite purpose.

Trainee: is a major stakeholder in a training program.

Trainer: is the person only who can remove the mental block of trainee, motivate the trainee to learn, delete the negative perception of the trainee regarding the training.

Task or role analysis: refers to a systematic and detailed analysis of jobs to identify job contents, the knowledge, skills and aptitudes required and the work behavior.

Training objectives: are some kind of statements of what training is expected to achieve

Training Evaluation: is the process of examining a training program.

V

Vestibule training: refers to the method which attempts to duplicate on –the job situations in a company classroom and utilizes equipment which closely resembles the actual ones used on the job.

Vision: tells that where the organization sees itself few years down the line.

Index

A

B

C

F

G

H

I

T

U

V

W

Z